Fling Open the Doors

Giving the Church Away to the Community

Paul Nixon

Abingdon Press

Nashville

FLING OPEN THE DOORS:
GIVING THE CHURCH AWAY TO THE COMMUNITY

Library of Congress Cataloging-in-Publication Data

Nixon, Paul, 1962-
Fling open the doors : giving the church away to the community / Paul Nixon.
 p. cm.
 ISBN 0-687-04554-1 (pbk. : alk. paper)
 1. Church growth. I. Title.

 BV652.25 .N59 2002
 253—dc21

2001007696

02 03 04 05 06 07 08 09 10 11—10 9 8 7 6 5 4 3 2 1

MANUFACTURED IN THE UNITED STATES OF AMERICA

Contents

Foreword

The local congregation is the primary mission unity of Christ's church in the world. This simple fact is the deep and exciting mystery that Paul Nixon unfolds for future church leaders. It seems so simple, so obvious, and so biblically clear . . . and yet so many churches, denominational judicatories, faith-based agencies, and benevolent community organizations consistently fail to grasp that truth.

Paul understands this truth. He also understands how the discernment of this truth can be so difficult for traditionally trained church leaders, and how stressful this truth can be for traditionally minded church participants. Strip away the membership privileges. Surrender the clergy prestige. Shoot the sacred cows. All that matters is the Gospel, and everything else is tactics.

The title of this book is well chosen. It gives you a clue . . . and a warning . . . to the point that Paul will drive home. The goal is not just to "open the doors of the church" so that the public will come into the holy institution, join the membership, support its programs, pay its salaries, and protect its heritage. This book is not about opening the doors of the church with an incremental, cautious strategic plan that will filter out the riffraff and draw in the right kind of people with the time, talent, and money to guarantee success for the institutional agenda. This book is about *flinging* the doors open. It's about passionately, daringly, kicking open the heart of the Body of Christ, so that the followers of Jesus can *get out* . . . in order to *do good* . . . and daringly articulate their *faith motivation for doing it!*

Therefore, Paul's own story of life and leadership is necessarily bound up with his recommendations for the reorientation of the church from maintenance to mission. The transformation of the leader's heart and the redirection of the congregation's mission energy go together. The tactics of one congregation may not be readily transferable to another context . . . but the power, principles, and mission focus modeled in Paul's church experience *are* transferable to any church, of any size, in any culture in North America. More than this, his experience verifies that "flinging open the doors" is not abstract or wishful thinking . . . but a genuine potential to multiply mission for any congregation. It can be done . . . *if you desire it above all else!*

Readers of this book will not only take heart, but they will find practical coaching. Paul has the rare ability to speak in ordinary language that makes sense to leaders of any age or background. He "connects" with people. He makes "eye contact" with the reader. He understands your position, and gently leads you to do practical things, which cumulatively fulfill a revolutionary vision.

Church leaders will experience Paul's story in much the same way as eighteenth century homesteaders heard Daniel Boone talk about Kentucky over the mountains. Like Daniel Boone, Paul has actually been there, and the vision of Kentucky and the story of the journey will run together. He has helped create the kind of church he is describing. He will map the best gaps through the mountains, mark the best trails to follow, and help you decide what gear to pack and what to leave behind. He won't minimize the dangers, but he can't help rhapsodizing the wonders of the destination. In the midst of all the practical coaching, you will never miss the gleam in his eye or the excitement in his words. So leave your tidy cottages and comfort zones behind, and let this explorer show you another way to be the church. The first step is the fling open the doors.

Thomas G. Bandy, November 2001

Introduction

There is a legend from the days of the 1917 Revolution in Russia. According to the legend, at the very moment when the Bolsheviks were marching through Saint Petersburg, the leaders of the Russian Church were engaged in a heated debate about the colors of the vestments for worship. Their society was in a crisis moment approaching meltdown, and the church was worrying about the most inward of concerns, pouring their passion into questions such as whether to wear purple or blue.

There is something about that story, be it fact or fiction, that rings chillingly true to any of us who have been church leaders for very long. It is so very easy for churches to become disconnected with the concerns of the wider community and world and to become obsessed with internal matters. Even churches with strong traditions of outreach and social justice can easily become abstract and issue-oriented in their relationship to the world, rather than focused upon the particular people who live in the shadows of their steeples, people with very particular names and needs, attitudes and personalities. It is so very easy to lose touch with the communities we are called to serve and to disciple.

If I have learned one thing about the relationship between churches and their communities in the years since I embarked on this journey of pastoral ministry, it would have to be this: *for a church to make a difference in the life of a community, it has to plant itself squarely in the center of community life.* This planting is more than simply a matter of building location. It is more than providing an array of "outreach" programs. It is something that must go to the heart the church's identity. The burning issues that drive the church forward must be issues that go to the heart of the community's needs. A church must understand that its constituency is not its membership. Members represent simply the inner circle of leadership. A church's primary constituency must be the wider community of peoples in which it lives.

At the same time, for a church to make a *real difference* in the life of a community, it must also offer something different than simply a mirroring of the community's values. The church must have a sense of purpose and good news that comes from God, enabling it to lead constructively in the renewal of people's lives. The church must truly believe that it has something to offer that the world cannot live without!

For the last nine years I have served on the pastoral team of Gulf Breeze United Methodist Church. During these years, our church has attempted *to become a community center* in the fullest possible sense. As a result of that commitment, our church has grown far beyond the pace of population growth in our area. Our community is located on a narrow peninsula of land on the Florida coast. The town of Gulf Breeze, Florida, itself is more an island than a peninsula, since it is surrounded by water on three sides and by national park land on the fourth. Population growth is slowing in our community due to the lack of additional land for development. Yet our church's growth has accelerated. The reason for this is found in the evolving relationship between our church and our community.

In this twenty-first century, I believe the battle for effective ministry will center around core values and behavior more than around theology. A church that *lives the values* of the good news of Jesus will thrive more often than not. A church *that lives in love with the people* God has placed around them will thrive more often than not. A church that is more concerned with preserving traditions than relating to unreached people will decline more often than not. A church that is more concerned with sharing correct ideology than in sharing hope will decline more often than not. A church that is more concerned with healing itself institutionally than with healing the lives of people will decline more often than not.

A church's street signage can tell volumes about a church. Many signs have changeable message boards located beneath the name of the church or business. Churches who have such message boards often waste this valuable communication opportunity with the passing public. They post such things as the names of their staff members or, even worse, cutesy sayings about life from bad email. Very often you see the pastor's sermon title for the next Sunday, perhaps alongside the words, "The fourth Sunday after Epiphany."

There is a church, not far from where I live, that regularly shocks me with the messages on its message board. About the time that our church was beginning a very nontraditional worship service in order to engage unreached peoples in our community, I noticed that this church changed the message on their sign to read, "A traditional (insert denomination) church." About the time that we were giving away easy-to-read Bibles by the box full, they posted a series of messages that read as follows: "Want to know what God says? Then get a Bible." "Have a Bible? Then read it." Once or twice the reader board advertised "Revival Services nightly." Over the months that followed, I noticed fewer cars at the church, and rarely saw any weekday signs of human life around their facilities. Their pastor left in discouragement. Then, not too long ago, I nearly drove off the road when I noticed the latest message on their sign: "Lord, send us the Lost!" And I thought to myself, "They have communicated almost every possible message to drive community people away, and now they post such a prayer on their reader board!" They represent many thousands of churches across North America who may have good intentions, but who have not yet figured out that in order to change a community, we churches first have to be willing to change ourselves, to change the ways we approach ministry, and to change our attitudes toward our unreached neighbors.

How can we change the relationship between a church and its community? How do we build an extroverted church that engages the interest and imagination of the wider community? What makes a church relevant? How does a church come to the place where it is truly making a difference in the lives of people who, otherwise, would never have a reason to set foot inside a church? How can we fling open the church's doors both literally and figuratively, in order to place our church at the heart of our community? These are the questions that have driven me in the writing of this book.

Prevailing churches in the twenty-first century will, more often than not, be intensely community-oriented. They will be marked by

1. a deeply felt sense of mission that compels them to reach out and make disciples in the spirit of the New Testament, without the polarizing theology so common among growing congregations in the twentieth century;
2. a view of their physical facilities as community centers for the peoples they serve;
3. an intense concern for connecting with the unchurched public, but never at the price of compromising the core of the faith as they understand it;
4. multiple locations for doing ministry;
5. a varied experience in church growth patterns: healthy and steady addition in some settings and explosive, combustive multiplication in others;
6. the willingness to change behaviors and strategies in order to bust through plateaus in numerical growth;
7. a team approach to ministry: multiple teaching pastors and ministry done by all the members.

Some churches will be called to be extreme in their message and approach. Most churches, however, are not so called. Those churches who have a more balanced self-understanding and a more diverse constituency may find it encouraging to know that the twenty-first century will belong more to them than it will belong to the more strident "our way or no way" church down the street.

In 1994, three key words were placed at the heart of our church's mission statement. They are the words, *hospitality, hope,* and *healing*. Since that time, God has steadily unfolded and revealed what these words mean for our church's ministry, even to the birth of our East Campus in 1999, and the opening of the Gulf Breeze Community Life Center. We have often said that the Community Life Center is a gift to our community. The most powerful gift, however, is not a facility of bricks and mortar, but the hospitality, hope, and healing that is offered and delivered through the facility. Chapter three, the longest chapter in this book, deals with these three themes. Hospitality, hope, and healing are foundational to all that is written in these pages. This stuff isn't pretty window dressing for us. It is the heart and soul that drives our church. It is in our DNA. Please do not skip over chapter three!

Chapters one and two share the basic experience from which this book is born. Chapters three and four deal with the conditions that are necessary for a church to effectively fling open its doors. Chapters five and six get into the nuts and bolts of community ministry, leadership development, and worship. Chapter seven deals with potential pitfalls as well as the price of leading a church toward an open-door ministry. Chapter eight looks to the future and to the application of these principles in diverse settings.

If you, the reader, reach a point in this book where you begin to feel overwhelmed, I encourage you to put the book down for a while. Just as we seek not to overwhelm first-time guests at our church with all that's wrong with their lives, I don't want you to be overwhelmed with all that's wrong with your church. The truth of the matter is that God can start with us at any point, and move us in the right direction in manageable steps. Even when we stand blocked by the Red Sea or a stubborn church governing board, God always has his ways of getting us to the places he is calling us to go. If God is for us, we have already won the victory.

The pages ahead tell a story. In one sense, this is autobiography. In another sense, it is a glimpse into the *playbook* of an outstanding ministry organization that now has a record of twenty-six consecutive winning seasons, at least as measured by worship attendance growth. However, the point of the story is not about a sleepy coastal community in Florida, any more than the point of the Christ story is about life in the Galilean hills of Israel. And yet, God's good news always seems to come to us *incarnate*, embedded in real lives in real places. Most of the things that I write on these pages, I learned in one particular church and community. I share the story because I believe it can serve to unlock some critical truths for many churches in thousands of communities.

My prayer is that the pages ahead might serve as inspiration for greater stories yet to be written, as twenty-first century Christian leaders take hold of the key values of Jesus and dare their churches to live those values in their communities. Dream with me here for a couple hundred pages. And after you have dreamed with me, keep dreaming with God, until God brings those dreams to life! Any church can become a center where all are welcomed, encouraged, and healed. Including yours.

CHAPTER ONE

A Village Church

Every church has a story. And every church has a village. Actually, every church has at least two villages. There is a geographical village, literally the neighborhood or physical community where the church's facilities are located. But more important, there is a virtual village that is not based on geography, but upon the people groups who are drawn together in a church. A church's story and its villages are intertwined. You can't understand one without the others. And certainly we can't talk about flinging open a church's doors until we take seriously both that church's story and the particular villages where that story is played out.

I serve as a pastor to a village church . . . and to several villages beyond that church. The first village beyond our church consists of about 30,000 people who live in the neighborhoods on our peninsula and in the adjacent beach community. About a fifth of the people who live in this region identify themselves with our church in some fashion. Our church understands that it belongs to all of the people who live in this community.

However, our church's virtual village transcends the specific neighborhoods near our church property. This wider village includes increasing numbers of persons who drive more than ten miles to share in the life of our church. Even as the traffic on U.S. 98 becomes more and more clogged with cars and some of our area residents begin to feel like they live in an Atlanta suburb, we are cultivating a virtual village, where people know one another's names and care about one another's lives. This virtual village is reaching far beyond our present membership and far beyond the typical church-going population. The common denominator for the people in this virtual village is that they have each experienced a sense of community through a ministry of our church and feel at home with us in some respect. For many churches in the next ten years, this sense of virtual village will increasingly rely upon Internet connectedness.

Within my church's virtual village, one finds many villages really. These villages form around diverse interests, ranging from indoor soccer to skateboarding to Bible study. In each of these villages, we work very intentionally to cultivate a climate of Christian hospitality, hope, and healing, and to invite participants to spiritual growth opportunities.

In this chapter, I want to examine the context in which my church lives. In order for you, the reader, to evaluate the relative applicability of the ministry principles that I am espousing in this book, you need to know where I am coming from.

People are people, whether they live in the Bronx or in Sioux Falls, whether they live in the suburbs of Toronto or in a beach community in Florida. And yet two churches can be based across the street from one another in the same physical neighborhood and be vastly different, both in their stories and in the villages they serve. No two congregations share exactly the same story or serve identical villages.

Our Story, Our Village

Our church, like many American congregations, was born in a geographic village of a couple hundred people. Thirty-eight years before I got there, Gulf Breeze, Florida, was simply a post office and a few homes situated in the jungle on a small peninsula of land out in the middle of Pensacola Bay. In 1955, opossums, skunks, and rattlesnakes each outnumbered *Homo sapiens* in our community many times over.

The village grew, and with it, the church. A larger bridge was built, providing easier access to shopping, health care, and bright lights. By 1975, the village had become a small city of about 5,000 people, now a bedroom community of commuters to Pensacola. Gulf Islands National Seashore had taken possession of all the land on the eastern border of the city limit, making the town an island, in practical effect. Very little undeveloped land remained by 1975. Population growth slowed to a trickle. The city of Pensacola Beach, located across another bridge to our south, had about 3,000 people by the mid-70s. They, too, were nearing saturation of buildable land. Future growth of the church would have to depend on something other than population expansion in a five-mile radius.

During these first twenty years, from 1955 to 1975, churches and schools remained squarely at the center of community life. During this era, our church grew to be a liturgically traditional, denominationally loyal, politically conservative, theologically moderate, thoroughly suburban United Methodist congregation—not unlike hundreds of others across the United States at that time.

These were the twilight years of an era in human history that had spanned many centuries; an era commonly called Christendom. It was an era that most folks consider reaching back to the fourth century when the Roman Emperor Constantine made Christianity the favored religion of the empire. Almost overnight, the separation between the church and the empire dissolved. It was an extreme event, a crisis for the church in many respects. Suddenly, the church faced the daunting task of trying to figure out who it was in a world where all citizens were tacitly members.

One of the marks of the Christendom era, especially in Europe, was that there were few outsiders to the church. Almost everyone was an insider, unless you were a Jew. You may have been lax in your church attendance and pagan in your personal life, but if you lived in the geographic region, if you lived in the physical village, the church in that village was your church.

A host of commentators ranging from Bill Easum to Lyle Schaller to Loren Mead have written about this era of history and the shift that has occurred toward a new era in our lifetimes. The world we knew until 1980 has passed away forever. Loren Mead, in *The Once and Future Church*, defines the shift that came to the church back in the fourth century with the birth of Christendom. With regard to the local church, he writes,

> "Under the Christendom Paradigm, the local incarnation of church stopped being a tight community of convinced, committed, embattled believers supporting each other within a hostile environment. Instead, it became a parish, comprising a geographic region and all the people in it. Everyone within the geographic bounds of the parish became *ipso facto* members of parish and church. No place in the local arena was seen as 'outside' the church . . . The parish pastor became a community chaplain, a civil servant and local holy person." *(Loren Mead, The Once and Future Church, The Alban Institute, 1991, 15-16.)*

Big, Bad Assumptions

In a society where you are, by geographical proximity, a member of the village church, several assumptions are made, some unconsciously. Some of the most common are listed below.

- *People are born into the faith.* They are Christian due to an identity stamped upon them at birth. They will be loyal to the church of their baptism their whole lives.
- *All of society's institutions (governments, schools, businesses, etc.) are founded upon and governed by Christian principles.* A person still living in the Christendom paradigm (way of looking at the world) may have difficulty distinguishing how the church, the Rotary Club, and the public school differ in their foundational principles and mission. God and country stand for the same things in Christendom.

- *Churches need to be more faithful to the forms, traditions, institutions, and values passed on by their forebears* than to the needs, desires, and hopes of the people they are called to serve. In the Christendom model, we expect people to tolerate and even embrace antiquated forms.

In reality, there has never been a time when these assumptions were fully true in any community. However, these assumptions are growing less true by the day in most communities. Church behaviors rooted in these old assumptions can form major impediments to effective ministry in a society that is rapidly losing its church-centered character.

Even after many decades of accumulating estrangement in North America between church culture and the mainstream of public culture, millions of Christian leaders still expect people to relate to God on the church's terms, in the church's language and within the church's sub-culture. We hold on to ancient language and terminology, awkward rituals, medieval dress, and antiquated discipleship strategies. Or we resist the kinds of experiences, music, and communication forms that will encourage spiritual transformation among today's teens and adults.

By 1975, the village that our church served was rapidly changing. Please read carefully what I am about to say. Our village in 1975 was undergoing a redefinition. In a society that decreasingly identified with us (the church) as its center, we decreasingly identified with the wider society. The primary village for the church was becoming its membership, and other friends and supporters who believed in its mission. This was not happening simply in one community. Over the latter half of the twentieth century, this had happened in thousands of congregations across North America.

Across the land, there were two basic church responses to the rapidly changing culture among mainline Protestants. There was our church's response, which we might call *privatization*, to essentially shift from being a community church to being a private club that serves the needs of its members and constituents. The other common response was *secular-ization*, to continue to serve the community, but to serve in ways that were increasingly secular. Typical of the latter response was the delivery of social services to the community without offering a compelling word for Christ or attempting to make Christian disciples of the people served.

Both of these responses to the end of Christendom have been disastrous for mainline churches. In one typical scenario, a church allows the village it serves to shrink to where it comprises only a band of dues-paying insiders. In the other scenario, a church might keep its community focus, but allow its mission to become secularized, serving the wider village, but offering only such things as food and job skills.

I should note that there are a whole family of denominations and churches who have sailed through the end of Christendom with less obvious trouble. In general, these were churches that never bought into the Christendom model to begin with. Throughout the last two generations, these churches viewed themselves as a bastion of the faithful in a world of unfaithfulness. For many of these churches, with a *church versus the world* mentality, winning the lost people isn't any more difficult today than in 1970. It was hard work then. It is hard work now. These churches often assume three key things: that the church has entirely different values than the world, values not open for much debate; that a person has to be essentially reborn to move from the world to the church; and that the church should constantly change its methods in order connect effectively with worldly persons and reach them for Christ. These churches have much to teach the rest of us about effectiveness.

Our church by 1975 had responded to the seismic cultural shifts of the day by subtly turning inward. A casual observer might have missed this altogether. After all, the church loyally supported denominational mission efforts. Members were happy to see new people join the church and share the workload and the financial obligations. In theory at least, they wanted to see their church grow and serve more of the community's people.

But their behavior gave conflicting signals. The doors of the church facility were usually locked, except for a few church-sponsored groups and activities. There was the usual apprehension about keeping the place clean during the week for church on Sunday. They were over-budgeted for their income, meaning that there was never any money for significant investment in outreach. They took care of their own. They tried to pay the bills, or at least most of the bills. They were stuck in Christendom.

A lot of churches are still stuck there.

There are churches, ranging from Southern Baptist to Roman Catholic, who still retain a strong enough internal culture that they have been able to preserve an illusion of Christendom. Most of their new members are church transfer. Suburban population growth, good marketing, and extremely high-quality delivery of ministry programs and services have helped these churches capture a higher percentage share of a shrinking market of people. These churches appear for now to be exceptions to the trends. However, I would expect that in the next quarter century, many of them will face major crises of identity and institutional decline as they come to look increasingly odd and out of date to new generations.

In most traditional congregations, the crises have been apparent now for several years. Steadily decreasing numbers of baptized children are seeking confirmation to church membership. My denomination's 1992 General Conference responded to this reality with legislation that, in effect, declared baptized babies to be full members. This legislation could have slowed or even temporarily reversed our membership decline. Our judicial council overturned it; nevertheless it represented a last-ditch grasping for the world of Christendom where babies were born into the faith. It represents a protest against a world where eighth graders look at our creeds, litanies, and choral anthems and collectively yawn, if they look at all.

Churches of quite divergent social and theological outlooks still spend enormous amounts of time and energy signing petitions, passing resolutions, and seeking to amend the laws of the land or to affect social change in the wider society. For the most part, these efforts affect very little substantive social change. Very often there is another Christian group working just as hard for the opposite cause, creating a stalemate of sorts. Churches often get involved in such polarizing campaigns because they are grieving the loss of Christendom. If only they could redraw the laws, they believe the nation would be compelled to at least act like Christians.

Perhaps the strangest grieving of the loss of Christendom can be observed in thousands of music ministry suites in North American churches. An extremely isolated ghetto culture of church music in the mainline denominations has all but lost touch with the popular musical movements of our time. In my community, I can find at least twenty radio stations on my FM dial, two of which are classical and a couple of which are Christian. Most of these stations would not touch any of the music that is being published for mainline church choirs these days. Over-intellectualized music has effectively killed the spirit of worship in thousands of churches for all but an elite few.

Opening Up Our Virtual Village

The first leadership task for Herb Sadler, the new pastor appointed to our church in 1975, was to try to open up the church's virtual village to include more people, without watering down our mission to nothing more than social ministry. About two months after he arrived in town, Herb preached a message from Revelation 3:7-8, focusing upon the words, "I have set before you an open door." He said to the people gathered that day, "We are going to open the doors. We are going to swing the doors open. We are going to be a church for everyone." That sermon turned out to be a watershed moment for our church. Over the last quarter century, we have opened that village up to the point that we now see ourselves as in mission to and with every person who lives on our peninsula.

This may look, to the distant observer, like Christendom all over again. It is not. There is no wishful thinking on our part that the people of our community care about the future of United Methodism or about the seasons of the church year. There are no assumptions on our part that the people of our community are already Christian or that all roads lead to heaven. Even though we consider ourselves to be in mission to and with every person in our community, we also understand that each of these persons needs to experience the transforming power of Christ. There is no attitude toward the villagers that they are welcome here only if they meet us on our terms, in our manner of dress, singing our favorite old hymns, etc.

Specifically, we increased attention to ministries and efforts aimed at spiritual transformation of youth and adults. We have focused first on changing lives before trying to change the world. And we have invested in a multifaceted music ministry that involves hundreds of people in a wide range of experiences, with a high value on the popular appeal of the music. Quite simply, we believe we ought to sing the kind of music that people like rather than the kind of music that professionals wish they would like. We are determined that our village is wider than simply the public radio crowd.

A community-oriented church in the post-Christendom world is marked by certain assumptions. These nine assumptions form what I will call "characteristics of a village church." They form the core values for this book.

21

Characteristics of a Village Church

1. The members understand that the church exists for the community and belongs to the community. In fact, they consider it a sacred responsibility to serve the people who live in their community. This community is usually both geographic and virtual. A geographic community, like the old parish concept, consists of the people who live within a certain territory that can be outlined on a map. This territory can be a neighborhood or an entire city: it is simply the geographic area for which the church takes special responsibility. A virtual community is the combination of certain people groups, which a church feels a special calling to serve. These groups may be distributed over a wide region. Most regional churches specialize in serving certain groups of people, whether they have formally defined these groups or not.

Once the church understands that it belongs to the community, the community itself will begin to figure this out as well. Realtors and psychotherapists who have never attended the church will begin to send folks there based upon the community perception/reputation of open doors and needs met. Community groups will naturally seek to hold community functions at the church facility.

2. The members also understand that the church transcends the village it serves. They understand that the village does not necessarily buy in to the church's values. They understand that the church's mission comes from God. They understand that the church has something unique to offer the village which can be found nowhere else. They believe that the people of the village and the people of the church all need the transforming power of Christ.

We can take seriously the reality that Christians are a minority in a secular society, while at the same time welcoming all peoples into our midst. This is just the opposite of the denial we see in many quarters. It is recognition that as the church becomes engaged with its community, and establishes itself as a center of community life, pre-

Christian people can begin the journey toward faith in the context of quality relationships with Christian people. A church can commit to offering pastoral oversight to a community without assuming that all the people in that community are believers.

3. *If the church owns a facility, it feels a special calling to serve the people who work or live in the surrounding neighborhood, especially the children.* Regardless of where the church's members primarily live, a village church takes neighbors near its facility seriously. It understands that it must develop ministries that serve its immediate neighbors, even if it is not primarily a neighborhood church. If the people who live nearest to us never experience an open door into our faith community, something is very wrong. If a church is unwilling or *unable* to minister to the people who live near its facility, it should prayerfully consider relocating and offering that facility to a group who is committed to serving the neighborhood.

4. *There are multiple ports of entry for peoples of the community to get into the church.* In a village church, it's easy to "get in" to church life. Diverse and life-relevant ministries are offered, designed around the needs and interests of community people, with intentional publicity and invitation extended to community people. From music, to sports, to social events, to community education and life coaching, there is something offered for nearly everybody. And once a person enters the church's life through a certain ministry, easy transitions are provided to more spiritually-focused activities.

5. *Ministries and activities are offered in the local time zone, throughout the week.* A village church is a seven-day-a-week church. It stays in touch with the needs and life rhythm of the people it wishes to serve, offering worship and activities at a variety of times so that everyone can participate. If there are a significant number of people in the village who work or who are unlikely to attend church on Sunday

morning, then worship services are likely offered at alternate times as well.

6. *Diverse peoples are brought together in community, healing the community's divisions, wounds, and prejudices.* There is significant ideological diversity in many of the prevailing churches of our day, as well as significant socio-economic diversity. A village church pastor seeks to help all these people move forward together, teaching positive themes and truths that enable spiritual growth in all. A village church knows that there is too much common ground in the Christian good news for us to need to spend time tearing each other down or splintering into factions.

7. *Worship occurs in ways that make sense to and touch the hearts of community people. Worship becomes a celebration of the people.* The worship ought, therefore, to be accessible and meaningful to the average Mary and Joe in the wider community. This is not to say we must ignore the sub-culture of the church membership. *It is to say that the needs of the church membership are secondary to the needs of those not yet reached with the Christian good news.* In the incredibly complex and diverse culture of twenty-first century America, most churches ought to be offering more than one type of worship service if they are serious about making worship meaningful and central to the communities they serve. At least one service should be decidedly non-traditional in form, designed with the wider village in mind.

8. *There is no difference in the treatment of members and non-members, nor is there any difference in their opportunities for participation in basic ministries and services.* A village church believes that the church ought to be a social, educational, recreational, and therapeutic center of life for its community. In such a church, a person does not have to be a member or profess the Christian faith in order to enjoy the church's services. Neither does a person have to be a member in order to receive certain opportunities to offer themselves in service to others. There will certainly be mandatory training and formal commitments necessary for

spiritual leadership in the church community. But there are no preferences extended to church members as far as access to services and programs offered. Where fees are involved with church activities, there is one fee for all, members and non-members (though scholarships may be offered on the basis of financial constraints).

9. *To join oneself to this church is to join oneself to the community, to commit to serving one's neighbors.* In fact, there is no reason to join such a church unless one wants to roll up sleeves and start serving others. A village church declares itself to be a spiritual home for all the people in its community. One does not have to transfer membership here in order to raise one's children in the church, to attend services or enjoy the multitude of activities offered. But when a person is ready to become a servant, then it is time to make a formal covenant with this church.

Over the past quarter century, our church has gradually come to reflect the nine characteristics of a village church listed above. Nothing was overnight. Change was incremental. Change has been painful for a few. But gradually, we embraced a gentle, hopeful, healing approach to the faith that set us apart from many congregations. Again and again, people who came to the church talked about never having been a part of such an uplifting place. And by the hundreds they came. Many were recovering addicts or recovering from family or personal trauma. Our church began to think of itself as a "hospital where everybody is recovering from something."

The Milestones

Key milestones in Gulf Breeze United Methodist Church becoming an effective village church

1975   Open Door policy instituted for community groups who wish to meet in the church facilities.

1976   A second Sunday morning worship service is offered, accommodating diversity of schedules and increasing usable space in sanctuary. This is a critical step in moving beyond a tight circle of insiders, as it now becomes impossible for members to know everyone.

1977 Alcoholics Anonymous begins meeting in the church facilities.

1981 Church becomes more global in its sense of village, with its first hands-on mission trip outside U.S. borders. This would expand within the next two decades into mission commitments and relationships on every continent but Australia. This marked a shift from paying others to do missions, to hands-on involvement with our neighbors.

1983 A 650-seat sanctuary built to accommodate the people not yet a part of us. Senior pastor surpasses seven years tenure. These two events signal a very different future for this traditional, mainline congregation.

1986 Under leadership of new youth pastor, the church's youth ministry acquires an adjacent building and the church establishes a reputation as the center of youth ministry for the community.

1988 Under leadership of the first full-time music director, the graded choir program is marketed aggressively as a center of community music education for children, with enrollments eventually soaring to over 400 area children and teens.

1991 Church becomes the first organization in the region to build a Habitat for Humanity House on its own. This ministry, which is slowly but surely building a small subdivision near our East Campus, has done as much as any other thing to help both our church and our wider village understand that we care about our community.

1991 Church begins a third Sunday morning service, concurrent with children's Sunday school at the 9:30 hour.

1993 Church begins a preschool to serve community families.

1993 Church forms a partnership with a group of persons in Satka, Russia, with the intent of starting a church. (Church started in 1999.)

1996   The 9:30 Sunday morning service moves toward a non-traditional format, with a quadrupling of adult professions of faith in the following six months, and a doubling of 9:30 attendance in the following two years.

1996   Church launches a small website, which could, within a few years, become the most significant thing on this list.

1997   Church decides to build a community center eight miles from its other facilities on a new East Campus.

1999   Under leadership of the first Director of Community Recreation, a recreation ministry is launched with over 2,000 registered participants in our database from the first year, the majority not church members.

1999   Church launches a fourth Sunday morning worship service (East Campus), with edgier music and a more informal style. Half of participants have been uninvolved in organized religion for more than seven years.

2000   Church launches a revamped ministry to youth and young adults called The Bridge. Fifth weekly worship service, called The Bridge, begins in January of 2001.

2001   Café 98, a large-scale food service for area residents, is launched at the East Campus on Thursday evenings.

During the last quarter of the twentieth century, our church grew from less than 100 in weekly attendance to more than 1,800. The growth line was remarkably steady throughout this period. The largest jumps came the first and last years in this time span, that is, just after Herb Sadler arrived in 1975, and just after we opened our East Campus in 1999. In most other years, the gains were relatively modest.

There were, of course, those who resisted the open door policy. They worried about the neighborhood children messing up the carpet. They worried about the kinds of folks that Alcoholics Anonymous might attract. They worried that sacred spaces would be disturbed. But over time, most people either bought in to the open door policy or they left the church.

A Critical Junction

By April of 1997, several indicators said that our church's growth had peaked. With an average Sunday attendance of 1,300 on five crowded acres with grossly inadequate parking, several new trends had developed: worship attendance growth had stalled and represented a steadily decreasing percentage of the total membership; key program ministries which had been significant feeders of people into our church were either in decline or were now significantly smaller than they had been five years earlier, including music ministry, youth ministry, and single adult ministry; and we had failed to acquire an extraordinarily valuable adjacent acre of land that had come on the market, even after we had offered approximately $800,000 for it, leaving us land-locked without reasonable hope of physical expansion.

One prominent exception to the bad news: the numbers of adults joining our church by profession of faith had skyrocketed since we had changed our 9:30 A.M. service to a less formal format with a praise band and drama team.

During the first six months of 1996, before the change, we recorded twelve adult professions of faith. In the last six months of 1996, we recorded forty-eight, most of whom came in through the 9:30 service. During 1997, total number of persons joining our church by profession of faith jumped to 163 for the year, more than half of our total new members. This very hopeful trend led us to believe that we could reach and make Christians of many more persons than we were presently serving if only we could provide additional space and ports of entry.

However, massive shifts were occurring around us that required more than simply expanding "church the way we knew how to do it" to another site. If our church was to remain the spiritual center of our community, major shifts in our ministry strategy would be required.

By 1997, the villages that we served had changed remarkably from twenty years earlier. There were now more two-worker families, more single-parent and blended families, more people without significant church experience as part of their history, more competing Sunday activities, more folks who owned no "dress clothes," vastly different musical tastes, and little or any loyalty to denominational name brands. There were also more people, more schools, more traffic, more hours at work. An increasing number of daily interpersonal contacts were with strangers.

Less and less time was being spent with family, with neighbors, or at church. The village of family was shrinking. Increasing numbers of persons had moved into our area, whose extended family lived hundreds of miles to the north. Thus the village of extended family had become a much weaker influence in daily life than anyone could remember.

The sense of village with physical neighbors was diminishing as well. In the mid-1990s, two hurricanes hit our area in the span of two months. As the eye of the first hurricane passed over, and the fury suddenly stopped, all the neighbors on my street cautiously ventured out into the street to survey the damage and to debrief with one another about the most incredible morning most of us had ever experienced. Though I had lived in that house for two years, this was the first time I had ever talked to most of these people. We laughed. We marveled at the downed trees. We borrowed batteries and supplies from one another. Turbines had blown off all of our roofs like projectiles, and we sorted out which turbine belonged to whom. Then in just less than an hour, the winds were again raging and we were all cloistered back within our respective fortresses. After we sawed up the downed trees in each other's yards in the following week, I would wave to those people occasionally as I drove past their houses. But in most cases, we would never speak again. This illustrates how much the geographic village, the literal village, has weakened as an influence in our daily lives.

Finally, there was a weakening spiritual village in our community. Quite simply, a decreasing percentage of people in our community were attending church. This was due, in part, to the fact that the regional population growth had greatly outpaced the addition of new churches to serve the people. More and more people were competing for seating and parking in a handful of vital churches. Also, we are a community of transplants from other areas. As people moved in to our area, many of those who had church backgrounds did not immediately search for a new church family. It has been typical to see folks wait five or more years to begin looking for a church if they look at all.

We have thus seen on a modest scale the same thing that happened as easterners migrated over the continental divide a hundred years earlier. Millions of people who had church connections in eastern North America lost those connections as they migrated west. To this day, church involvement as a percentage of population is typically lower in the West and in communities that have been, at some point, populated by large migrations of people from other regions of the nation.

By creating a community center on our East Campus, we made a choice to address the shrinking sense of village in our area. It was a choice to serve the geographic village, to address our neighbors in terms of their perceived needs. But we also wanted to provide a place where the needs they do not yet perceive could be met in an equally effectively manner. It was a choice to strengthen the spiritual village in our community. In chapter five, we will examine the ways in which we created community around recreational interests and moved these people into a spiritual village. The creation of this new community center was also a way to defy and exceed the limits that had been placed on our church's growth by lack of space at our Main Campus.

Your Story; Your Village

What is your church's story? Probably it intersects with my church's story in certain ways. Certainly it diverges in other ways. Who are the people in the villages that your church serves? They may be older or younger than the people in my church's villages. They may have different cultural or ethnic identities. Is there a significant difference between the people in your church's spiritual village and the people in the geographical village around your facility? If so, has your church's leadership considered entering a partnership with other community leaders, and even other pastors, to interact with the people all around you?

If I were to go to the public school nearest to your church's facility, would the principal describe your church as an ally in his or her work? If I were to ask for directions at the convenience store two blocks from your church's facility, could the clerk tell me how to get to your church? Would they have ever heard of your church? If I were to buy a home near your church, would the realtor be able to recommend your church as a place conducive to life quality in the community, perhaps citing some ministry or community service you offer as part of her strategy to sell me the house? If I moved into that house, within a mile of your church's facility, are there reasons that I might find myself walking in your doors, other than entering to worship God? Perhaps I'd find a public school event, a forum of candidates running for sheriff, an Alcoholics Anonymous meeting, a Saturday morning indoor soccer game, or an evening computer class offered by the community college. Or would I ever find a compelling reason to walk through your church's doors?

And if I walked through those doors, how would I feel once I was inside? Would I have entered a place that is bright and inviting, furnished tastefully but simply, with well-designed bulletin boards, fresh paint, and carpet?

Would the signage and greeters speak to me in my primary language? Would I see other people that looked like me and dressed like me? Would there be opportunity for me to discover other activities, ministries, or services offered in this place that might bring me back another time? Would I see or smell food? Would there be a chance to grab a bite to eat before I left?

Increasing numbers of churches are sensing that they can thrive without owning a building. Nevertheless, most churches will continue to be landowners in the near future. And every one of those landowner churches sits on a continuum somewhere between a fortress on one extreme and a community center on the other extreme. Where is your church on that continuum? I believe the closer we can be to the community center end, the better chance we have of serving the people God has placed around us.

Most established churches, however, are closer to a fortress than to a community center. And many other churches that offer their facilities to the community for secular events have yet to discover effective ways to use such events as a port of entry into their spiritual village.

But, what if?! What if more churches came to believe they had a sacred responsibility to serve the people who lived in the various villages around them? What if the members of those churches came to understand that their church belonged to *all* those people? What if worship were celebrated in those churches in ways that are truly indigenous to the variety of people out there? It would mean that the church would reassume a mantle of community leadership and influence that has been lost with the passing of the Christendom era. A network of village churches will not recreate Christendom, nor would we really want it to. But such a network will plant the Christian church squarely in the middle of community life for millions of people who presently live untouched by the good news of Christ.

A church's choice to remain a fortress is a choice to withdraw from the fray of life in the twenty-first century, to withdraw to the margins of society, to leave millions of people to quasi-Christian cults, Eastern religions, and secular paths of salvation. It is to say to the people we are called to serve, "We don't care about you."

Your church will soon come to a crossroad of decision, if it is not at one already. What will you do? Circle the wagons? Consolidate the losses? Find a younger pastor? Spend a couple million on a pipe organ? Or will you take seriously the requirements for effectively serving your neighbors?

It may require a lot of work and money. It did for us. The first phase of our community center cost us $4 million over and above our regular ministry costs, plus the additional costs of doing ministry at the new site. The funding and construction often necessary for such a ministry expansion will add hours to the workweek for a church's pastors and administrative staff. It will add thousands of dollars to the annual financial pledge for hundreds of a church's families.

In our case, we were already a large church with the ability to offer high quality ministries to our church families. Growing this church larger was not really a direct benefit to these pastors, staff members, or families. So why did we do it?

We did it for others. We did it for neighbors. Some of us did it for generations of young people that we would not even live to see grow up. We did it because we wanted to make a difference in the lives of those kids and in the life of our community fifty years from now. We did it because we believed that for a church to truly be a church, there had to be a "giving away" of the church to the community.

Jesus taught us that when we seek to save our lives, we lose them, and when we give life away we gain life. If this is true of individual lives, certainly it is equally true of the life we share together as a church. A lot of the thinking about church growth and congregational renewal in the last twenty years has been motivated by a concern to save our present congregations and denominations as institutions. And so we feverishly study ways to attract baby boomers or whomever the case might be, seeking to keep the doors of our churches open for another decade, another year, another Sunday. But, then, after all our learning, we come to a crossroad where we must decide if we are willing to do the things necessary to reach the next generation or the newest people group in our communities. One road before us means choosing to change and give up some of what we have personally held as meaningful in order to reach others. The other road means business as usual and decline.

Churches regularly come to crossroads, where, each time, we have to decide if we really want to let go of what we have so that God can offer his blessing and love to others. In more than one instance, our church has chosen to give a large part of itself and its resources away to serving its neighbors. As a result, it has reached a lot of new people, many of whom have never before been part of a church. In the latest influx, we are tapping into a group of folks who wouldn't know the Gloria Patri from a gourmet dish at an Italian restaurant. And we aren't teaching it to them either. Many of these new people have never held a United Methodist hymnal in their hands, and most of them would recognize less than five songs out of seven hundred. Few have ever knelt at a carpeted rail for communion. But these people are encountering Christ. Their lives are being transformed. Their hands are getting inside Bibles for the first time ever. These newcomers cannot tell you the name of even one of our church's seven founding members. But they have caught the vision of what those seven people sacrificed to create. And they are excited and ready to share the love of Jesus with others and to invite their friends to church.

A few years back, I was consulting with a group of church leaders about what it would take to reach their community. Everyone was nodding and smiling like they usually do at such meetings. Finally, I just took the whole bunch on a walk out the door of the fellowship hall and down the street. We walked about a mile. Several of them had never been on the streets we walked or seen any of the tidy mobile homes. I asked them, "Do you really want to serve these neighbors?" In the weeks following that consultation, the pastor and some of the leadership at that church planned and proposed a community center, similar to what we built but on a much smaller scale, to be located between their present facility and a public ball field. The plan was doable and could have brought hundreds of their neighbors in contact with their care and ministry. But in a close vote, that church decided to table the plan.

The same band of folks are still worshiping there, sitting on the same pews, minus the ones that have died. The people on the ball field still come and play and leave, never even seeing that there is a church next door. The folks inside the sanctuary continue to express and celebrate their faith in their accustomed ways. The kids on that ball field could go from playing tee-ball until the day they coach their grandchildren, and never have a clue what that church next door to their ball field is all about.

Across the street from most Christian sanctuaries are neighbors who are honestly clueless. And most churches forgot about those people years and years ago. Fifty years ago, as Episcopal priest Sam Shoemaker reflected on this reality, he made a new commitment to remember the people across the street:

> I admire the people who go way in.
> But I wish they would not forget how it was before they
>   got in. Then they would be able to help
> the people who have not yet even found the door,
> or the people who want to run away again from
>   God.
> You can go in too deeply, and stay in too long,
> and forget the people outside the door.
> As for me, I shall take my old accustomed place,
> near enough to God to hear him, and know he is there,

but not so far from people as not to hear them,
and remember they are there, too.
Where? Outside the door—
Thousands of them, millions of them.
But—more important for me—
One of them, two of them, ten of them,
whose hands I am intended to put on the latch.
So I shall stay by the door and wait
for those who seek it.
"I had rather be a door-keeper . . ."
So I stay near the door.

—Sam Shoemaker

Our church decided we would fling open our doors, not to recreate the across-the-street neighbor in our own image, but rather to establish community with her, to offer a place where he can be himself, to offer a place where both she and we can both be transformed. We risked losing things with the doors wide open, and we have lost some things. But what we gained is so much more precious than what is lost! We gained brothers and sisters. We gained the joy of knowing that we came to the crossroad, and went the right way.

It may be that your church is ready to open up its virtual village, to enlarge the variety of people that you serve. It may be that this book can function as an inspiration to your leadership to think creatively and pro-actively to move forward in making your church a village church. If you sense such a readiness in your church, give thanks to God! And move quickly to rally your leadership in bold mission to the wider village. You should seize the opportunity, made possible by your church's spiritual readiness, and move boldly to plant your church as a spiritual and social center for a wider community of God's children.

Looking Ahead in the Virtual Village

In the early years of the twentieth century, with the advent of radio, the nature of the virtual village began changing for a few churches. Churches began using airwaves to carry their message to places far beyond face-to-face reach, and far beyond a day's journey. Certain enterprising pastors multiplied many times the number of folks exposed to their teaching. Other pastors and churches, my church among them, threw all of their energy into face-to-face encounters. The primary reasons that my congregation stayed out of radio and TV broadcasting are the financial cost, and the belief that it is better for folks to find a face-to-face gathering of believers where they can develop the fullest sense of community. We believe that the good news takes on flesh and makes its maximal impact as it is experienced alongside and through relationships with other people.

An ad sponsored by the Episcopal Ad Project echoes our sentiment. The black and white newspaper ad features a TV outfitted like a communion table, with candles on top and a preacher on screen. The caption reads, "The sermon may be pretty good, but when was the last time he served you Holy Communion?"

However, that ad, and the related negative attitude toward broadcast media, is about to become obsolete. Broadcast media is becoming interactive. Interactive media, via the Internet, is fast becoming entirely different from the mere talking heads of TV. Now, and in the world that is fast approaching, people can and will talk back. A real community is forming on-line that reaches across language, culture, and geographic region.

In this new century, Christian chat groups and email listserves are already establishing virtual communities with only the simplest of boundaries. In just a few years, conferencing technology will enable millions of virtual villages to grow up around affinities of every sort. The relationships established, the accountability discovered, and the meaning experienced in such groups will be as significant as if the people were physically gathered together. The possibilities for a Christian community to be available to a person will soon be exponentially greater that what it is now. Such a community will be available at any hour of the day or night. No longer will someone's quirky personal schedule prevent him or her from going to church.

Imagine a big-screen TV divided into half a dozen screens, with the faces of various group participants engaged in live, real-time discussion or study. Imagine groups formed around incredibly specialized affinities, such as mothers of children with a certain rare disease. You might have a woman in New York, another in Florida and one in Paris and another in Jakarta. Before this group was formed, each of them felt all alone in their stress and grief. And yet, through the Internet, they will find one another and form a Christian support group, just as if they all lived on the same block. Meaningful interaction will begin taking place between persons who live on different continents, with powerful friendships forming that transcend oceans, languages, and political systems.

Language differences will be erased by software that instantly translates French to Spanish, English to Russian, Italian to Chinese. In just a few decades, such virtual villages may become the primary spiritual communities for millions of people.

In a few years, we will move from two-dimensional talking heads on big screens to three-dimensional images of entire bodies right there in the room with us. Persons from every continent will be instantly available to sit with us in our homes, drink coffee, study the Bible, pray, and share their lives with us. Obviously, this communications revolution raises enormous opportunities and challenges for churches.

The day will soon be over when any class or group needs to be defined by geographic neighborhoods, or be limited to those who can gather at 9:00 A.M. in little rooms behind the sanctuary. The possibilities will be endless. And the Christian worldview will not be the only game in town. Our grandchildren will face a marketplace of religions, lifestyles, and ideas that is simply beyond our imagination.

I mention all this simply to illustrate that the villages our churches serve will no longer be limited by geography in the twenty-first century. We need to think broadly and pro-actively in terms of the future of the spiritual villages we seek to create. We have to become anticipatory, to see where needs are heading and how resources are developing. In those instances where we continue to build buildings, we need to design them around very physical activities, around the things you can't yet do with a computer modem. Churches that offer quality athletic opportunities, good food, and lots of hugs will likely continue to have facilities full of people for many decades to come. Churches who serve extended villages of people *and who know how to disciple to those people* will prevail in the years ahead. Those churches will become the spiritual leaders of the twenty-first century world.

CHAPTER TWO

A Gift to the Community

The Recovery of an Old Idea

The concept of a Christian community center is certainly not new. One hundred thirty years prior to the opening of our Community Life Center, the New York City YMCA erected a similar building (constructed in Manhattan in 1869—the first of hundreds around the world). The Young Men's Christian Association began twenty-five years earlier as a movement emphasizing the development of body, mind, and spirit. Originally conceived by George Williams in London, England, as an organization to spread Christianity, the movement became decidedly secular in the twentieth century, maintaining its spiritual identity only in terms of a continuing interest in social justice issues. American YMCA facilities became essentially private recreational clubs. Whereas once prayer and Bible study were as much a part of YMCA life as recreation, today it would be a stretch of the imagination to think of one's local YMCA as an organization devoted to the spread of Christianity. My guess is that if George Williams were alive today, he would feel more in tune with what is happening at our Community Life Center than in what is happening at our area YMCA.

By the beginning of the last century, church-based community centers were springing up all across the United States. Especially between 1900-1920, American churches experienced a groundswell of concern about poverty and the sufferings of the poor. There were numerous voices that helped to raise this awareness and concern, but none more eloquent than Walter Rauschenbusch of New York.

Walter Rauschenbusch was a Baptist pastor who began his ministry in a Manhattan neighborhood of immigrants called Hell's Kitchen. Struggling with the issue of Christian response to urban problems, Rauschenbusch articulated a theology of social action early in the twentieth century. The most famous of his books, written in 1917, is entitled *A Theology for the Social Gospel*. Building on the foundation begun by George Williams, Rauschenbusch taught that saving souls is a war that is waged on multiple fronts. Believing that people were indivisible units of body, mind, and soul, he taught that the social and physical needs of people must be met alongside their spiritual needs.

Many of the Christian community centers founded in North America across the twentieth century still serve their communities in creative and constantly changing ways. Most have, like the YMCA movement, become almost entirely non-evangelistic in their ministry, focusing not only on recreation, but also on concerns such as literacy, food, medical needs, and child care. Several of these centers, such as Wesley-Rankin Center in West Dallas and Mobile Inner City Ministry in Mobile, Alabama, also serve as the meeting place for Christian congregations who seek to invite persons served by the center to hear the Christian good news and share in a Christian community. There are a handful of community centers, such as Glide Memorial United Methodist Church in San Francisco, which are operated entirely as the ministry of one congregation, serving as a conduit through which people in the community are invited to be wholly incorporated into the life of the congregation.

These Christian community centers have typically been cooperative ministries of several congregations, either of one denomination or one neighborhood. And almost all of these centers have been located in poor neighborhoods where social problems were most acute.

During the '60s up through the '80s, there was a resurgence of interest in such community centers as a method of church extension. However, there have been very few new congregations planted via community centers which have thrived. Where thriving congregations have been connected with thriving community centers, investigation will usually discover a very strong core of spiritual community that existed prior to the development of the various community ministries. These spiritual communities, which become the sponsors of the broader ministries, provide the sense of soul and anchor the mission of the community ministries.

During the latter half of the twentieth century, thousands of U.S. churches have built recreational facilities, commonly deemed Family Life Centers or Christian Life Centers. Once built, the vast majority of these facilities have been understaffed and underutilized. Even where such facilities have been actively used in ministry, the facilities have been used primarily to serve the church members and their families in an age of growing affluence. The location of these family life centers has typically been adjacent to the church's sanctuary and educational facilities. People who would feel hesitant to walk into the sanctuary would feel a similar hesitancy to walk into another building in the overall church complex. Almost none of these facilities were built to serve community needs. In many of the congregations, as the numbers of youth in the church has declined, the usage of the family life center has declined as well. (There are some happy exceptions to the above paragraph sprinkled around, but very few.)

An "Ah-hah" Moment

Something happened on April 3, 1997—something that seven people will never forget. We were gathered for lunch in an upper room, the upstairs dining room at Michelle's by the Bay, a restaurant overlooking Pensacola Bay. The sun was sparkling on the water; it was a thoroughly gorgeous spring day on the Gulf Coast. We broke bread together, we laughed and shared. At first it was simply a delightful lunch gathering of six leaders from our church with Ken Callahan, a outside consultant helping us to think about the future of our church's ministry. But about halfway through our two hours there, the wind of the Holy Spirit began to blow in that room.

It was Callahan's second visit with our church. I had picked him up at the airport the day before. No sooner had we crossed the three-mile bridge to Gulf Breeze, he said, "Before we go to the hotel, swing me over by the church, just around the block once." So we detoured a couple blocks off of U.S. 98 to see the church campus. As I turned the corner, I pointed out a building the church had acquired after his last visit. He was more interested in the sanctuary. He said, "You have added on." "Yes," I replied, pleased that he had noticed, "we added about 250 seats a couple years ago." Then he asked, "How much parking did you add?" "We didn't add any parking," I said. He paused. The car sat idling in the middle of the street. Finally he said, "Let me get this straight. You added 250 seats in the sanctuary, but you didn't add any parking?" "That is right," I said sheepishly, beginning to see his point. Again he said, "You added 250 seats but you didn't add any parking." "Yep," Mercifully, he dropped the subject. I went on to share that we had recently attempted to buy an adjacent acre for an outrageous sum of money but had failed. I told him that a realtor in the church was gathering data on all adjacent property and who owned it. He was uninterested. He asked, "Is there a ten acre tract of land within five miles of here?" I replied that land was scarce on our peninsula, but that we would check. He said, "Good. We will want to look at that land tomorrow."

He then opted to postpone the hotel, and we spent the next couple hours in a little café on Pensacola Beach. While we were seated there, he pulled out a demographic summary that I had written on the population trends in our church's area of ministry. He asked, "Who wrote this?" I said, "I did." "Well it's all wrong." "It is?" "Yes, it is." He proceeded to inform me that I had led with negative information in the report. I had begun by reporting that the population growth in the area immediately around our church had ceased and that the median age of the community was rising. He stopped and asked, "Do you believe your church's best days are ahead of us or behind us?" "Ahead of us," I replied. "Well you would never know it from this report. Lead with the possibilities!" he said. "Lead with the possibilities!"

What, exactly, were the possibilities for a congregation that had utterly overgrown its landlocked five acres, a congregation that was already, by some measures, more than half the size of its hometown, a congregation whose center of ministry was surrounded by water on the tip of a tiny peninsula with negative population growth?

Stay and Go

The next day, our eyes were opened to the possibilities. Callahan looked around our lunch table and asked us where we might find the nearest available ten-acre plot of land. Phil Sandfort, the chair of the church's board of trustees, responded that he had recently been made aware of such a plot about eight miles east of the church's present campus. Callahan's eyes gleamed. "Buy it. Get a contract. Don't delay. Start today. Work out the administrative details later."

The land Phil referred to had good highway frontage on U.S. 98, the major traffic corridor of our region. It was located a mile from a new Super Wal-Mart and a mile from a new bridge that would be built within the next two years. Ironically, the price of the land was $800,000 for *thirteen* acres, almost exactly the price of the *one* acre we had been unable to purchase the previous month.

We responded to this proposition by saying that our church had an excellent location already, poised at the intersection of three communities. Callahan responded, "I am not suggesting that you should abandon your present location. I am suggesting that you should stay at your present location *and* go to a new location. Stay and go. At the new location, you can build a recreational facility in which you can serve thousands of area residents. It would be a gift to this community. You can also begin a fourth Sunday morning worship service there."

The words "gift to this community" burned on my ears. I glanced around the room and I saw that each person present had immediately caught the vision of what we could do. The East Campus of Gulf Breeze United Methodist Church was born that day in that upper room. But more important, a key principle was verbalized. This principle had already been at the heart of our church and was responsible for much of our church's growth in the '80s and '90s. The principle? That our church should see itself as a gift to our community. (Note: The first unit to be built at the East Campus was a 43,000-square-foot facility called the *Community Life Center*. For the next few years, the Community Life Center would be the only building at the East Campus. For the purposes of this book, the terms East Campus and Community Life Center are interchangeable.)

For years, we had flung open the doors of our church's facilities to community groups, to recovery fellowships, and to ministry projects serving various people groups seven days a week. But in April of 1997, the principle became more explicit to us than ever before. With the building of our next facility, we would move from being a church that was open to the community to being a church that was, by design, a community center in the fullest sense.

Over the previous two decades, our church had gained a reputation as a community-minded church, growing steadily, to the point that we ran out of room for any further growth on our five-and-a-half acres of land. By the mid-90s, our weekend worship attendance had all but stopped growing, and was stuck at about 1,300. As we looked around the state of Florida, we found a dozen other United Methodist congregations stuck at about the same plateau, and none who had, as of 1995, broken through that ceiling. The events that occurred as a result of that upper room meeting on April 3, 1997, would finally break that ceiling for us and propel us toward our destiny as a church that exists first for others.

Like a Whirlwind

Within a week of that fateful luncheon, we bought the land. It happened like a whirlwind. Before detractors could stall the purchase, our trustees bought the land. We reasoned that land was appreciating and we could always sell it if either our church's administrative body or the denominational committee controlling church planting and expansion did not approve the plan. It was a cash purchase, due to a gift from a member's will and due to the fact that the church had accumulated some savings from several years of budget surpluses. Since we did not have to take out a loan, the purchase was faster than it might otherwise have been. No loan had to be approved. Nobody had to vote the church into debt. Until this time, I had sometimes felt that our church was a bit too conservative financially. However, the church's propensity to save enabled it to have the resources to seize a once-in-a-lifetime opportunity quickly when it came. Had we waited longer, detractors would have had more chances to derail the project. I am convinced that had we not been in a position to move quickly that we would have lost the opportunity.

Most churches who have accumulated resources are afraid to spend those resources in bold missional investments. For those churches with a propensity to save for a rainy day, I would simply point out that had we left the money in savings, bearing little interest, we would have missed the opportunity of the church's lifetime. There *is* a time to save. But there is also a time to raid every cent for the sake of the mission. I thank God that we came upon a vision and a project that propelled us to divest ourselves of accumulated assets for the sake of God's mission.

The community center concept was not really controversial. It was a natural extension of who we were as a church. However, building the thing on a piece of land eight miles removed from our Main Campus *was* somewhat controversial, a very new way of thinking about the meaning of congregation, not limited to one ministry center. Negotiations were required both with the local denominational committee on church location as well as with a neighboring United Methodist congregation, Saint Paul Church, whose location was just under two miles from our proposed East Campus.

In our denomination, a regional committee must approve the location and building of church facilities. This committee initially responded to our East Campus proposal by expressing fear for the future of Saint Paul Church. However, after considerable conversation, the committee saw the wisdom in what we were seeking to do.

In many such district committees across our denomination, the simple fact that our proposal involved a site within two miles of another United Methodist congregation's property would have killed the deal. Too often, such decisions are driven by in-house denominational politics rather than by what is in the best interest of God's mission and the local community in question. We have a tendency to treat our existing churches like franchises with territorial rights, even when most of our churches reach only a tiny fraction of the people in their area. In our denomination, as in many others, *turf* is a concern that often muddies the waters of the most important issue, which is to consider which course of action will enable us to reach the most people for Christ. Had it not been for the dialogue our church initiated directly with Saint Paul, it is very possible that our proposal would have never been permitted by the denomination.

The hardest sell, however, came at home, back at Gulf Breeze Church itself. There were many people in our church who immediately saw the vision, understood what we were attempting to do, and appreciated the wisdom of it. But there were many others who felt threatened by it or simply could not see the wisdom of it.

Many hours of listening and responding to concerned church members was required in order to allay various fears. For a few, highly vocal individuals, it became a deeply emotional issue, probably due more to the process of quick and decisive action rather than the usual months of deliberation that most established churches are accustomed to. Churches often deliberate such issues until the nay-sayers and controllers have an opportunity to derail the plan. Had we waited until everyone was done talking before we purchased the land, we almost certainly would have lost the necessary momentum to accomplish such an unconventional thing.

When the votes were counted, a solid ten percent of our people remained squarely opposed to the expansion. However, despite this, I am unaware of any single member who left our church over the issue.

The Vision Catches and Spreads

Finally, it was the compelling nature of the vision that enabled our people to look past anxieties about one church operating in two locations. It was the strength of this vision that enabled the district committee to unanimously approve the project, despite its close proximity to Saint Paul. At the heart of the vision, Callahan's words echoed, "You are going to build this as a gift to the community." Though it was very clearly a church extension initiative, it was not a new church. It was simply a new center of community life, a place to address the needs that no one else was addressing, to fill the gaps in terms of community needs, especially the needs of children and youth. At the heart of this vision was the provision of a safe place for young people in an age where growing up was increasingly dangerous. This compelling vision wasn't *for* us. Nor was it *about* us, nor even about our denomination. It was about God's mission and the wider community. Many older adults in our church invested heavily in a project that would benefit themselves only modestly. Nevertheless, they wanted to plant a tree that would provide shade for generations to come.

People outside our church were quick to catch the vision. During construction in 1999, the *Pensacola News Journal* called me for an interview related to a story they were doing on growth and construction in south Santa Rosa County. Three of us met the reporter at the construction site in early June, and the next day a color photo of our construction site was on the front page of the newspaper. Why? Because it wasn't just another church under construction, but a community center designed to serve thousands of south Santa Rosa County residents. This story then caught the attention of the *News Journal*'s community editor, who was impressed that a church would build a community center. She allowed me to write a column, enabling me to interpret the project publicly, framing it as a community center rather than simply a church facility.

Then, at the grand opening, we decided to invite our local congressional representative to cut the ribbon. His appearance that day brought the newspaper back again, generating yet another major story, this time on the front of the local section, complete with a color picture of the congressman cutting the ribbon alongside our district superintendent and building committee chairman. The cost of all this excellent newspaper coverage was $0.00. We received this coverage because we were not perceived to be building a private facility, but a public facility. Once the newspaper caught the vision of "a gift to the community," they became an ally, helping us to communicate this truth with the wider community.

On September 12, 1999, when the doors of the Community Life Center opened officially, hundreds of community people came to celebrate who had previously had no connection to our church. Over the course of that week, we estimate that 3,000 people from the community, about half of these from beyond our church family, came through our doors and helped us celebrate our grand opening. Having accomplished this task, the battle of establishing a strong ministry at our East Campus was won. We offered an attractive facility and quality programming based upon demonstrated community need and interest. Once we got that many people in our doors, success was virtually guaranteed in every endeavor we would attempt there. We effectively taught our community that this new place belonged to them.

We Don't Need Warmed-Over '60s

Some folks may look briefly at our Community Life Center and see just a warmed-over version of the social action strategies that were common among mainline churches in the '60s and '70s. They may say, "Ah, I understand this. I've seen all this before." I would tell such a person to slow down and look a bit more closely. The main differences between this and many of the community centers that churches have built, especially in the inner city, would include the following:

1. Our center is operated by a single congregation rather than by a denomination, a congregation with a deep passion for reaching unchurched people and a proven track-record of leading them to faith. This arrangement provides for a strong sense of local ownership and accountability for the quality and success of ministries offered.
2. Our center has a dual purpose of creating spiritual community and serving the community's various social and recreational needs. Neither of these purposes overwhelms the other. This dual purpose is

reflected in facility design, in scheduling and facility usage, and in staffing.

3. Our staff, paid and unpaid, are indigenous to the neighborhood and culture(s) in which the center operates.

4. Our staff, paid and unpaid, are all on board with the motivation behind the center, to lead persons to a relationship with Christ. Evangelism is in our DNA.

5. Our paid staff are hard-working and extraordinarily competent in their respective fields. This reflects the value of excellence, one of the core values of our church.

6. A worshiping congregation is being built at the center who will soon, by their tithes and offerings, cover all ongoing costs associated with the center. In other words, the operation of the Community Life Center will be entirely self-funded. By the year 2002, we expect that all costs will be covered by programmatic user fees and by contributions collected in worship services held in the facility. The ministries will not be draining any mission dollars from the denomination or even from the Main Campus of Gulf Breeze Church.

Neither Do We Need Warmed-Over '80s

In the late twentieth century, American churches threw up recreational centers by the hundreds each year. Most of these facilities were simply fellowship halls with basketball hoops attached to the walls. Many were very extravagant in design; others were quite simple. Most were understaffed and underutilized. Most of these facilities were designed primarily to serve the families, especially the children and youth, within the churches who built them. Few were perceived as public facilities, either by the people who built them or by the neighbors who lived near them.

Perhaps the most common name for such buildings was *Family Life Center*. A few churches opted for *Christian Life Center*. Both of these names communicated that the facility so named existed primarily to serve the Christian families who worshiped in the sanctuaries just across the parking lot. We wanted people to feel comfortable coming here even if they did not feel a part of a traditional family and even if they were not Christian.

At one family life center that we visited during our building design process, an elderly woman was posted at the front door next to a sign for neighborhood school kids that read, "This is a church, not a place to hang out. It is for the use of our members and their guests." That family life center was blissfully empty that afternoon, being used by a solitary seventy-year-old man on a treadmill. Few churches are so brazen as to post a sign keeping outsiders out. More often, such facilities are simply understaffed and, therefore, locked up with the lights out during prime weekday hours.

I do not recall seeing one human being actually using the recreational facilities at any of the family life centers we visited, one of which served a 6,000-member church. More than one center was locked and dark in the middle of the day, forcing us to search for someone who would open up to let us look around.

Twenty-five years ago, I remember my father's chagrin that his home congregation in Lake Charles, Louisiana, had spent a million dollars to build one of these family life centers. When he went to see the place, the only thing going on there was a room full of older church women making cornshuck dolls. A quarter century later, that same church sold their property, family life center and all, to move to a *better* neighborhood. Had that church caught a vision for using their recreation center to serve the wider village as a community center, they might have built some bridges with a changing neighborhood over the next two decades and avoided the need to move.

Very few of the churches which have built family life centers have grown numerically in the wake of the untold millions they spent on these facilities. Many of these churches, however, have grown older and shrunk in size, leaving a smaller congregation to pay utilities and upkeep on a recreation building built for children who are now out of college and living far away.

The key differences between our Community Life Center and many family life centers include the following:

1. Our center seeks to provide recreation for the whole community, not simply for the community of Christians. We do not sponsor or host church leagues where, for example, the Baptists play the Presbyterians, or where church attendance is required to play ball. If we sponsor a league, it is a community league in which all community people are invited to register, not just those already participating in the life of an area church.
2. Our center is not located on a piece of land which includes a sanctuary or traditional church facility. Though it is owned and operated like a church, a person can come onto the property without feeling like they are at a church.
3. Our center is staffed eighty hours a week.
4. Our center was not built as *the youth building*. It belongs to everyone. On Sunday evenings when several of our church's youth fellowships are meeting eight miles away, the Community Life Center is serving all ages.
5. Our center is located on a major traffic artery with high visibility, not hidden on a side street or behind another church building. As of this writing, some 38,000 cars pass by daily.

In each of these points of difference, the key issue is the strength of connection established between the spiritual village and the larger village. In most YMCA programs, and in most family life centers or inner-city ministry centers there is a very weak connection between the spiritual community and the larger community that is served. People may receive various services and yet not discover easy or natural links toward involvement in a spiritual community. Or the sense of spiritual identity may be high, but little is offered that engages the interest or participation of the person outside the spiritual community.

When we began the Community Life Center project, our vision was to provide a center of community life for Gulf Breeze, Florida, with Christ at the center. For us, "Christ at the center" was more than a Christian mission statement on a wall plaque, more than church members on the board of directors, more than the church's name on the side of the building. For us, the vision was that a spiritual community might be based in a community center, and that the community ministries would be an outflow of the spiritual community. At the same time, we wanted the community ministries to provide ports of entry for people into participation in a spiritual community.

As we surveyed the needs of people in the community, we found a need for youth and adult team sports facilities, aerobics, walking and fitness activities, a preschool, afterschool programs, senior adult activities, and community group meeting space. We also found that an increasing number of the peninsula population were not church-attenders, demonstrating a clear need for new options and choices for Christian worship. So we proceeded to design a place where we could meet each of those needs. Had we been locating a community center in an inner-city location or in a more secular city, the primary needs may have been very different. In designing a community center, a church really needs to pay attention to the demonstrative needs in its unique community.

In keeping with what we learned about our community's needs, we blended the concept of community center and church facility. It became our goal to offer a center of community life for the residents on the eastern end of our community which would also double as a second center of spiritual life for a growing church. This required a new way of thinking for all of us, both within the church and outside it. Most of the thousands of people who walked through our doors in the first year came to the Community Life Center for something other than what you normally go to church for. Most of these people do not consider walking through our doors as "going to church."

Designing a Facility

It is important that, as churches build facilities of any kind, they link up with architects who are able to listen and think outside the box. In so doing, churches will want to avoid two critical mistakes: the mistake of limiting themselves to yesterday's facility designs, and the mistake of thinking all church-sponsored activities have to happen within the facilities they build. It was especially important for us to avoid these pitfalls, since what we were trying to do was really outside the established norms.

Standardized plans and layouts often reflect habits of church and community life that are from another day and another place. This is as true with worship centers as with buildings that support recreational ministry. Initially, we hired a site planner who specialized in designing family life centers. His opinions and categories of thinking were colored too heavily by his past experience. I am not sure he was ever able to really grasp our unique vision. As a result, we could never quite seem to fit all the things we needed into the 27,000 square foot box that we felt we could afford. The differences between what God was calling us to do and the typical family life center became clear to us. We needed to begin, not with a standardized plan before us, but with *a blank piece of paper!!!*

No church can facilitate everything they are called to be and do within a building. God will always call your church to do things that will never fit into your facilities. In our case, we lacked the necessary land to develop ball fields. We also lacked the space to adequately house our community ministries that offered food and clothing to people in financial difficulty. So we built what we could, with the understanding that some things would have to happen in other places.

Even the activities that we planned to do on site at the East Campus basically saturated the facility during prime-time hours in less than a year. With every building design we considered, including the one that we finally adopted and built, we said, "We will outgrow this in less than a year." And we did. This made it all the more important for us to move into the Community Life Center understanding that ministry would happen in many places all around the clock in our community. And it has.

A good local architect, George Koper, helped us in the following ways:

1. Rather than beginning with his preconceptions, he listened to our vision.
2. He pushed the gymnatorium from the center of the building to one corner, greatly reducing the amount of square footage wasted in hallways, effectively doubling the multi-purpose space available in the remainder of the building.
3. He was able to work constructively with the contractor in order to keep costs well below construction industry norms through simplicity of design and accommodation to pre-engineered materials wherever feasible.
4. Because of such cost savings, it was possible for us to shell in a second floor with an additional 16,000 square feet in the first phase of construction.
5. Even with such constraints, he still designed an attractive, brick facility, which was enhanced with excellent landscaping.

Avoiding Common Building Mistakes

Most church facilities suffer major flaws in design and usage. Among the most common flaws are that

1. too many rooms have only one use, which means they often sitting idle except for one or two hours a week;
2. too many rooms are controlled by one person, very often a Sunday school teacher or a choir director;

3. too few rooms are expandable and contractible in size;
4. halls and lobby areas tend to be too small and too dark;
5. where there is multi-purpose space, too much re-arranging of furniture has to happen from event to event, gobbling up too many labor hours in set-up and take-down. As a result, the staff and/or volunteers get tired and under-schedule the multi-purpose space.

Perhaps the biggest reason we have been so satisfied with our building layout at the Community Life Center is because we kept making changes, even during construction. We probably went to the architect and contractor two dozen times with minor adjustments to the blueprints several times during actual construction. In each case, we narrowly avoided mistakes.

For example, offices came as late additions to the floor plan. We had originally planned to have two offices, one for the recreation director and one for the children's ministry team. However, some of our church's lay leadership expressed concern that we needed more of our church's staff based at the East Campus. These people knew from business experience with multi-site organizations that every site needs adequate on-site management. So we carved two offices out of classrooms and turned the music suite into a Studio that doubles as office space for up to three persons. We turned our first aid room into an office. Finally we redesigned the office work room to allow for desk space and Internet access for any of our Main Campus staff while they are on site at the East Campus.

These additions required moving walls, changing floor treatments, altering electrical plans, and more. Many of these changes happened *during* construction. We were designing our ministry even as the building was going up. In a few cases, the latest word did not reach the appropriate people in time and we had to tear out cabinetry and redo it. The alternatives to this rather sloppy approach would have been to wait a year until we had done more extensive study or to just live with a building that was outdated from the day we moved in. We chose to make changes during construction. The patience and good attitudes of the architect, contractor, and building committee were essential to the process. Certainly the changes presented a challenge that many would consider frustrating. However, the final product was well worth the messy process.

I cannot overstate how important good communication skills and a flexible, can-do attitude are for architects, contractors, and building committees. Our architect had been named architect of the year by the area contractors the year before we built. This, plus the fact that he had built a similar building with an even more bare-bones budget the year earlier, convinced us that our architect could help us build what God was calling us to build for what we were able to pay.

Critical Considerations in a Community Building

The following issues are extremely important in the creation of winsome public buildings.

1. There should be a large, bright lobby area. This may be the most important room in the building. First impressions are made here. More people pass through this room than any other in the facility. Ideally, this lobby will have a glass wall enabling the passing traffic to see into the building. Conversation areas with wrap-around sofas and a large, centrally placed, U-shaped welcome desk are essential. A lobby should be a happy room, where people feel immediately at home upon entering. Hotel industry standards today demand that for every two square feet devoted to auditorium style seating, one square foot should be allotted for lobbies and atriums where people mix, mingle, and network before and after.

In our facility, we also have game tables and snack machines in one portion of the lobby, underlining the recreational mission of the building. I wish that our lobby were twice the size it is. Lots of windows help. I do not believe that we can overstate the importance of lobby/atrium type space in public facilities.

2. The larger the room, the more important that it be extremely flexible and multi-purpose! Study any large arena that is operating in the black and you are likely to discover an array of different kinds of events being staged in the main room, ranging from conventions to concerts to sporting events to public ice skating. Churches need to be learning from this!

Worship areas can double as gymnasiums, dining facilities, and concert halls. Advances in acoustical treatments and flooring materials make it possible for one room to serve a variety of high visibility functions. Dual lighting systems can enable brightness needed for athletics and the subdued ambiance needed for worship services. Installing two lighting systems is much, much more cost and space efficient than building two separate spaces.

At our Community Life Center, the gym can be transformed from an indoor soccer arena to a worship center in about ninety minutes on Saturday evenings, and into basketball readiness in about thirty minutes after Sunday morning services. Because the chairs are not bolted to the floor, we can change the seating configuration according to the needs of particular services. We can mix table seating and row seating according to the preferences of the people who attend a service. In our community, newcomers to Christian worship tend to like being able to sit at a table toward the back with a cup of coffee.

Our stage area is quite compact, with extensions added for concerts and worship services. Due to the extensive use of candles in our worship, we use uncarpeted stage extensions.

3. Every room is ultimately multi-purpose, except restrooms. Off the back hallway of the Community Life Center, we created five large multi-purpose rooms. Three of these rooms are attached to each other by movable walls, opening into a large room which has been used for the following and more: parties, aerobics, wedding receptions, elegant dinners, weeknight worship, conferences, retreats, Scouts, community groups, and a children's carnival. This triple room can accommodate up to 150 people for a breakfast or dinner, while recreational programming is under way simultaneously in the gym. One of our values in construction was to build a facility in which we could do multiple kinds of ministries simultaneously. On Sunday mornings, our elementary children's ministry uses the triple room for Sunday school and children's worship.

We call one of our multi-purpose rooms "the Studio." It is a music rehearsal area for various groups, a video editing center, a mid-week storage area for some of the sound equipment, and a bright office area. In the center of the room is a large, round table which serves as both dinner table and meeting table for various ministry teams on a daily basis.

But the concept of multi-purpose extends even beyond these rooms. Every room is multi-purpose, except the restrooms. This includes the pastor's office. No one owns any room. We are committed to using as much of our space as possible as many hours a week as possible to do ministry.

It is best, we have found, to have different kinds of multi-purpose space that is somewhat specialized from room to room, so that basic room set-ups can remain in place in many rooms. In other rooms, there can be a carefully defined range of set-up possibilities. Or, events which require a certain set-up can be scheduled back to back in the same rooms to minimize set-up and take-down time. In addition, cleaning and room set-up can and should happen after public hours as much as possible. Occasionally, we have had huge Saturday night events in our gym, which left our set-up crew working at two in the morning to make the room ready for Sunday worship a few hours later.

It is still usually more cost efficient to pay many years of labor costs in set-up and take-down than to acquire the land and build the facilities necessary to eliminate such labor. To put this in terms that typical Boards of Trustees understand, churches get a lot more bang for the buck by building multi-purpose space and staffing for set-up and take-down.

4. *Food service is not a luxury, but a basic necessity.* People need to eat. Moreover, they like to eat. Christians have been breaking bread together for twenty centuries. Facilities for preparing, serving, and eating food should be a part of the plan for almost any church facility. Kitchens are the most expensive room per square foot in most church facilities, and yet they are essential to our mission. It is important to look hard at a church's needs before over-building a commercial kitchen. It is equally important to examine those needs before under-building in this area.

Some churches are experimenting with food courts, where food is prepared by multiple outside vendors, similar to what happens at the mall. Malls feed people, in part, because they know that will extend the total length of shopping time the average person spends at the mall. Churches, likewise, should take advantage of every opportunity to feed people. Facilities should be designed so that food service can occur simultaneously with other high profile events.

In constructing such facilities, kitchens can run costs through the roof. Our building committee tried to steer a middle road, building enough kitchen to support ministry, while choosing simplicity whenever possible. We could easily have paid twice as much for the kitchen without having enhanced ministry and programming at all.

5. *Get as much space as possible up to code for child care usage.* Each state has different building codes relating to space that is legal to use for child care (where people are paying us to care for their children). It may not be in your church's immediate plans to use most of your facility for child care, but it is much simpler and cheaper to take care of such concerns in the initial design and construction than to try to retrofit the facility later, often after such codes will have become even stricter than they were to begin with. It may be that some rooms will only be used a few weeks a year with a day camp program, but you will be glad that you spent a little extra to get your space up to code. In the

future, a church may build additional space and then wish to expand its child care ministries in the older space. The church's future leaders may rise up and call you blessed for your having thought ahead to get the older space up to child care codes from day one.

The preschool children's area should have direct access from the building to the outdoor play area. There should also be a separate entrance for parents dropping off children that is apart from the main building entrance. The drop off area should allow for cars to drive through, so that children can be efficiently delivered back to the parent at the end of the day by the teacher to the car, without the parent ever parking or getting out of the car.

6. *Think multimedia everywhere.* Any worship area being built today should be designed for a large, rear-projection video screen (or two). Classrooms and lobby areas should be wired for high speed Internet connections as well as closed-circuit broadcasting. Even if a church has not yet developed the use of audio-visuals in worship and classes, we have to remember that we build facilities to last fifty years. And any building without such multimedia capabilities is going to be obsolete in the twenty-first century from the day the doors open.

7. *Keep office areas efficient and convenient.* The day of the acre office is past. The pastor's office at the Community Life Center is ten by ten (100 square feet), and it is the largest office in the building. Two of our key staff have offices that are off of the lobby. Another office is in the lobby at the welcome desk. Still another office is in the music studio. Two of our staff share an office. Too many churches eat up ministry space with administrative functions.

Whenever I have needed to meet with more than two people, we have simply moved the meeting outside my office. There are plenty of places in the world to meet with people, ranging from other rooms in our church's facilities to the Waffle House. I spend perhaps only a quarter of the time in my "office" that I spent ten years ago. With a laptop computer that can access email practically anywhere in the world, voice mail, and a cell phone, the world can be my office.

Staffing Is as Important as Roofing

People would think we were nuts if we started to build a building, but we planned so poorly that we ran out of funds before we got to the roof. The building would be essentially useless without a roof. In most cases, it is equally useless without a staff. When a church is budgeting for a new facility, it is important to include the anticipated start-up cost to do ministry in the facility. Most of this cost will relate to staffing the facility.

Churches build facilities all the time without setting aside resources to adequately staff those facilities. They tell themselves, "We will pay off the building debt first, then hire the staff." Or they say, "We will hire one this year and add another next year." Or they say, "We will add staff as the ministry grows." As a result, beautiful new buildings sit empty, pristine and unused. This is a terrible waste of the investment God's people have made to build these buildings in the first place.

Until we plant the seeds of outstanding staff leadership, the growth will likely be much slower than it otherwise would be. Our church's leadership chose to staff the East Campus for as fast a ministry start-up as possible. The tremendous success enjoyed by all ministries in the first year is a direct result of our commitment to put up the money to pay for excellent staff leadership. This up front financial investment in staff and programming costs was every bit as important for us as the financial investment of building the Community Life Center in the first place.

We realized that to staff a new facility, there would be a significant leap in the size of our church staff during the year 1999, with a corresponding spike in the cost of our payroll. One way in which we blunted the impact of the sharp increase in staff cost was to split this increase over two budget years; that is, we started most of the new positions in the middle of a fiscal year, meaning that the total impact was not felt until the year 2000. Nevertheless, the size of our program staff (pastors and full-time ministry directors) doubled between 1997 and 2000. Our payroll and related expenses increased by sixty percent during the same time frame.

At the outset of 1999, we planned on six full-time staff at the East Campus in addition to preschool staff and hourly workers in recreation and childcare. By the end of that same year, we had ten full-time staff instead of the six we had planned. Six of the ten were pastors or ministry directors. According to the traditional formula of one pastor/director to every 100 in worship attendance, we were staffed to support an attendance of 600 in East Campus worship from the day we opened our doors.

The two most critical new positions for us were (1) the worship/music pastor who would help to develop the new worship services, and (2) the director of community recreation who would mobilize leadership and participation from far beyond our church membership in a variety of recreational endeavors. To have waited on adding either of these critical positions would have delayed the development of our ministries. To have hired the wrong people for either of these two positions would also have set us back many months in the development of our ministries and in the growth of our church. Both of these challenges required nation-wide searches for the right persons.

In many cases, it may take two years or more before new ministries are entirely self-supporting financially. At the end of the first year, the offerings from our new worship service were underwriting approximately half the total monthly costs associated with the East Campus-based ministries, with reasonable expectation that the Community Life Center would be entirely self-funded by 2002. Our preschool and recreation programs, each of which charged user fees, were already in the black after one year.

Send Them a Positive Sign

Signage says a lot about an organization. It is worth investing in signage that has high community visibility and that sends a positive message, even if such signs have to be located away from the church property. Such signs should always be at the upper end of the size and quality range when compared to other nearby signs on the same road.

With all the increased expenses in our 1999 budget surrounding new staff and start-up costs at the East Campus, there were some things that got cut from the church budget. One cut was a proposed billboard along U.S. 98. Thankfully, however, one of our members was the CEO of a company that had a lease on several area billboards. That company subleased one of these billboards to us at no cost for three months. The only cost was printing the paper and hanging it. About two weeks prior to our grand opening, and for many weeks afterward, a bright yellow billboard shouted daily to tens of thousands of passers-by the question "Are you having fun yet?" and invited them to the Community Life Center.

Finally, the $10,000 brick sign and message board in front of the Community Life Center, though late getting built, has been perhaps the greatest single public relations instrument our church has ever found. The sign, which can be read from both east and west-bound lanes of U.S. 98, is constructed of a quality that places it in the top five percent of signs along U.S. 98, both in size and aesthetics. Because we change the messages daily, people continue to read it daily.

Some basic rules for our highway message board are to:

1. not have moralistic, judgmental, negative, or cutesy sayings about life;
2. invite the public to activities and events designed with them in mind, things we know they would like to do if they simply knew about them;
3. change the message on each side of the board daily, even if it means moving a message from one side of the board to the other and back again;

4. seek to vary the kinds of events publicized, and the types of people served;
5. occasionally print a word of celebration or congratulations that is relevant simply at the community level (such as welcoming a new middle school to the community the week they open their doors or congratulating an athletic team in the community that has won a championship).

Sometimes, to save money, churches put up signs at their construction sites that are so unprofessional that it would be better to have no sign at all. In the months following the construction of the Community Life Center, there was another beautiful church facility under construction next door to us, identified by a crooked, hand-stenciled sign on scrap wood. That sign did not tell the truth about that congregation. Nevertheless, for as long as it was posted, it broadcast some pretty pointed messages to the community.

1. We are a small, struggling congregation.
2. We are not committed to quality in our ministry.
3. We are unprepared to meet your needs or your family's needs.
4. Go to the church next door.

By the end of construction, that church next door had a beautiful sign, better landscaped than ours. They ceased communicating any of the above messages. And they began to grow.

Your Grand Opening Ought to Be Grand

About ten months prior to our grand opening, we convened a public relations team from within our church to tell the story of our new community center to the residents of our area. This team asked for $20,000, but was given only $10,000 for their tasks. That $10,000 was to cover all advertising related to the opening of the new facility, excluding the cost of a highway billboard and the actual cost of the grand opening events themselves (food, drinks, decorations, etc.).

We learned that you can indeed conduct a massive ad campaign for $10,000, but it isn't easy. There are ways to stretch advertising dollars so that you get back in value many times over what you spend. There are ways to save money without diminishing the effectiveness of communication. There are people in the church and community who will help you get the word out once they catch the vision of what you are seeking to do. Finally, if God is in it, weird and wonderful things will happen.

In our case, we were able to print some of our brochures in-house without compromising a quality look. We commissioned one of our staff members to spend about half the summer of 1999 making PowerPoint presentations to area groups, clubs, and businesses about this new facility and what it offered the community. We bought an ad in a local business magazine and were featured in an article in the same magazine in the following issue. Unable to afford three consecutive mass mailings to build visibility in our community, we chose to mass mail one piece, to stuff another in our local newspaper, and to hand-deliver a third piece as a door-hanger. Each piece was designed and written entirely in-house and printed by a local print shop. Our fledgling video production team produced an eight-minute video inviting people to our grand opening. We gave 200 copies of the video to anybody who would promise to give the video away to someone who was not a part of a church community. Finally, the local newspaper gave us extensive free coverage, including a front page story with color photos. The reason the newspaper was willing to do this was because we were not perceived to be building just another church. Rather, we were building a community center, a gift to the community, and that was newsworthy.

As a result of all this good publicity, about 3,000 attendees walked through the facility's doors during the eight days of our grand opening celebration. About half of these were guests. Few churches ever see 1,500 community people drop in to check out a new building. The difference was rooted in the fact that this was a community center, not just a church building.

Event	Attending	Guests
Grand Opening Brunch and Ribbon Cutting	1,400	400
Bob Carlisle Concert (first Sunday night)	850	400
Walk-ins off the street Monday— Saturday	400	300
Community Luncheon for Seniors (Wednesday)	300	120
Children's Night (Thursday)	100	20
Youth Night (Friday)	100	30
First Worship Service (second Sunday)	590	300
Community Picnic (second Sunday night)	600	300
Total Cumulative through our doors	4,340	1,870
Individual persons (estimated)	3,000	1,500

Back in 1997, Ken Callahan challenged us to get 3,000 persons through this building in its first year. As you can see from the above table, we met that goal in the first eight days. It would be difficult to overemphasize the importance of effective public relations in establishing such a ministry to the community.

But I should also relay the scariest part. We staged a gigantic grand opening week in a building that still had no written occupancy permit. The construction was in process down to the wire, and the permits were bogged down in bureaucratic county offices. We did not want to miss the momentum which a September opening would give. So we proceeded into a very stressful start-up week.

In an ideal scenario, we would have moved in and lived in the place a couple months prior to Grand Opening. This would have provided time to get the bugs out of the building before stressing the facility to its capacity several times in one week. People who are experienced in opening large public facilities know to build in a little time to "make sure all the toilets flush." In our case, the toilets actually stopped flushing during Grand Opening Sunday, causing sewage to back up all over the building, smelling bad, ruining the carpet in my office and causing enormous stress for all involved.

If we had it to do over again, would we push so hard on grand opening week? Our building was four months late being completed. It was the second Sunday in September when we took possession. However, as mid-September has been proven in many places to be the best time of year to start a new service, the answer is *yes*, I am sure we would do it again just the way we did. I would definitely recommend setting a target date for building occupancy that leaves up to six months as a margin for error. But in the end, if you lose five of the six months through construction delay, it is best to just deal with the stress, trust the Lord, and go for it.

It had been our dream all along to get a celebrity for our grand opening, a Christian entertainer, someone to create a buzz and draw a crowd. Unfortunately, we discovered they are all very expensive and booked months, even years, in advance. I had given up on the celebrity idea, until one day, a month before the grand opening, a member of the public relations team called me with an idea. Her sister worked for a Christian relief organization called Food for the Hungry. Food for the Hungry contracts with certain Christian artists to do benefit concerts for them in churches across the nation. As it turns out, grammy-winner Bob Carlisle (of "Butterfly Kisses" fame from 1997) had been booked for another church on our Grand Opening Sunday and the booking had fallen through. The only cost to Gulf Breeze Church would be $500. Would we be interested?

We cut a deal in about two hours from the time she called. Food for the Hungry checked out as a very fine and reputable organization. They provided all the publicity in exchange for the opportunity to make a low-key appeal to attenders about sponsoring children in a certain barrio of Lima, Peru. In the end, 850 people came to a fabulous concert complete with three video screens in sync with the music. Forty children were sponsored through Food for the Hungry. And our sense of community was extended to Lima, Peru.

The All-Important First Year

During its first year in operation, a Christian community center should capitalize on its new-kid-on-the-block status and play host to as wide an array of ministries and community activities as is humanly possible. In our case, these events fall roughly into four categories, each building upon the presence of the others, which are (1) ministries that directly advance the kingdom goal of making disciples; (2) ministries that meet a community need and serve as a conduit toward deeper involvement with the church; (3) services and activities sponsored by other community organizations, in keeping with our mission, which are held in our facilities; and (4) other community groups and events which simply rent space for their activities.

Under the first category, we would include Sunday worship, Bible classes, support groups for widows/widowers, divorce recovery, a camping/backpacking ministry, a women's support group, Christian concerts, large-scale ministry events for high schoolers, children's ministry events ranging from Vacation Bible School to weeknight children's discipleship ministries, middle school fellowships ranging from drama to skateboarding, Christian weight loss ministry, financial stress management classes, etc. These ministries are run by us and provide a direct Christian witness to the participants with the purpose of inviting them to place Christ at the center of their lives. Many church facilities are devoted exclusively to such activities. People generally come to these events looking for spiritual direction and/or growth opportunities. These are the kinds of things that might safely be categorized as "going to church."

The second category of activities meet a community need and offer an opportunity for relationship building, which can lead participants who are unchurched toward greater involvement in activities like the ones listed above. Our rec leagues, preschool, summer day camp, art classes, men's big-screen Monday night football, community picnics, and weeknight food service all fall into this category.

During the first year, our community recreation ministry included three indoor soccer leagues, two basketball leagues, three different types of aerobics, martial arts classes, two volleyball leagues, square dancing, karate, and clinics co-sponsored with a local university. These community services are offered for minimal registration costs to all the persons in our community—no strings attached. In addition, there are forty hours a week in the gymnasium and around seventy-five hours a week in the game room and fitness room when anyone could use the facilities free of charge.

The third category of activities reflect an open door policy toward community groups who could be partners with the church in meeting community needs. Such groups, not sponsored by our church, but welcome in our facility would include Alcoholics Anonymous, the American

Cancer Society, the American Heart Association, Lutheran Social Services, foster parenting classes, Hospice workshops, medical screenings, senior adult services and activities, defensive driving classes, etc. A local hospital uses our center for training events with hundreds of employees. The high school prom, the middle school band concert, and the elementary fifth grade graduation ceremony have all been held in this facility. During the 2000 football season, an area high school team ate dinner and relaxed in the building before games each week. We even shared space with a Presbyterian congregation who were without a home until their building was complete. They worshiped rent-free in our center for ten months.

The final category—community groups that simply rent space for meetings—have, for us, included a private employment agency, several area homeowner associations, the United States Department of Census, bridge clubs, and a host of private parties. The local Board of Realtors has rented our whole building for area gatherings of hundreds of real estate professionals.

I share the above details to offer a brief snapshot of how such a center can bring thousands of community people a year onto the church's turf. Just in our recreation leagues and activities alone, some 2,000 different individuals registered for at least one activity in the first twelve months we were open. Add their family members who come to watch them play, plus all the people in the other activities listed above, and you have several thousand people coming onto our turf. The Community Life Center is becoming a major center of life for our community. The vast majority of the people who have come through our doors are not yet a part of our church. Nevertheless, with this kind of traffic in the facility, is it any wonder that 590 people showed up for our first worship service on September 19, 1999? The enormous traffic flow in the facility has been one of the major contributing factors to the planting of this new worship community.

Five months after our grand opening, we baptized fifty adults in a single Sunday worship service. Two years after the grand opening, weekly worship attendance is steadily growing, from the low point of an average of 333 in December 1999 up to an average of over 500 in Fall 2001. About three-fourths of the crowd is new to our church. About half the people who attend worship at the Community Life Center on any given weekend were a part of no organized church one year earlier. East Campus worship is offered in a casual, non-threatening way in sync with the beach culture. People feel comfortable inviting their friends.

Because of this center's success in bringing so many onto our turf, our church gained a golden opportunity for spiritual influence in the lives of our community's people. Scores of people are now making professions of faith in Christ and getting connected with the Body of Christ because of this unique place.

When Is a Second Campus a Good Idea?

We probably could have raised more money in 1997, had we proposed to build something on our Main Campus, geared toward the persons who were already a part of our church. But we chose instead to build something for the people who were not yet a part of us. We chose to do ministry geared primarily toward those same people. We chose to give a gift to our community.

The decision to transition to a multiple-campus ministry was the right decision for Gulf Breeze Church for the following reasons.

1. We needed more space.
2. Neither relocation nor significant facility expansion was a viable option.
3. We already had a significant base of membership in the area where our second campus was proposed.

73

4. Our Main Campus continued to offer a valuable and strategic location for ministry. It is central and its neighborhood is stable.
5. We felt that we would be able to provide competent pastoral and staff leadership at two locations.
6. High trust existed among our pastors. (Had this not been the case, it might have been necessary for Herb to lead services at both campuses each week.)
7. We were large enough to be able to commit resources and staff to a "full service" ministry at both locations. (A church with less than 300 in worship would be well advised to think twice before spreading out onto two campuses, unless the second campus is very limited in cost or it represents the first step toward an eventual relocation of the Main Campus ministries to the new campus.)
8. Each campus would have certain features the other did not have, creating an interdependency between campuses. (The Main Campus has no recreation facility or dining hall for more than 200 people. The East Campus has no sanctuary or chapel. For certain types of functions, all members have to go to either one campus or the other.)
9. To have done nothing would have flown in the face of our mission and would have signaled to God, to ourselves, and to our community that we were beginning to retreat.

One of the biggest down sides of spreading out ministry across a community would be the amount of time that paid staff spend in transit between sites. Communication between staff is also more of a challenge over eight miles than when we are all together in one big cozy office suite. But thankfully, Alexander Graham Bell solved this issue for us a hundred years ago.

However, there are also great benefits in a two-site arrangement. It brings ministry closer to many people. In contrast to the few staff now traveling back and forth between sites, hundreds of others are being saved a trip to the other side of town, since they can find the ministry they are looking for at the site closest to them. This saves people time, enabling many to participate in a ministry or activity when they otherwise would not. In addition, by having the community center away from the building with the steeple, people are less likely to view the community center as a church fellowship hall, and more likely to view it as a public facility. As a result, more people are likely to enter the community center.

A Bridge from Secular to Sacred

The most basic key to the success of the Community Life Center is the way in which it has, in fact, bridged the secular and sacred. It has served as a connector between the spiritual village and the wider village. This center has bridged secular and sacred in the following ways.

1. It has enabled us to approach people holistically, to begin with them in one life arena (say in terms of a recovery group or a soccer league) and build relationships with them that raise their openness to experiences of spiritual community (activities such as worship or a small group formed for prayer, Bible study, or interpersonal spiritual support).

2. It has invited people to play in a place where they can come back and worship. Many of the people who feel most comfortable in a recreational facility are the same folks who feel least comfortable in a traditional sanctuary. With our model, they are able to make themselves at home in the space, raising the likelihood they would be comfortable returning to the same spot for worship. In most activities held at the Community Life Center they are likely to meet someone who attends worship there.

3. Even in worship, playfulness continues, coffee is served, and an environment is cultivated in which decidedly secular people can relax and enjoy themselves. Newcomers are commonly surprised how pleasant and fun the experience of worship can be. Worship ambiance and music is indigenous to the community. People feel at home immediately.

4. *People discover spiritual community in a place that doesn't smell like church, sound like church, look like church, feel like church (in certain ways), or taste like church.* For people who don't like church, and there are a lot of them, this is a good thing. For those who are really into the old songs and the old ways, we offer more traditional services for them every week at Main Campus. (As the style of worship that we do becomes more common in our region and across North America, we could gradually lose this advantage over the next decade. A continued commitment to quality and authenticity will be very important.)

5. *The worship ministry and discipleship ministries were planted simultaneously alongside the recreational and social ministries.* Both groups of ministries were present from day one, each feeding the other. High investments of funds, staff, and energy went to both sides from the outset. There was never a chance for people to start thinking of the Community Life Center as *just* a church or *just* a social services center. It was always more than simply one or the other, by careful design.

6. *The church's deep-set convictions about hospitality have helped to create a safe zone for seekers who are exploring the faith.* We provide a hospitable place for them to explore Christianity while allowing them space to be anonymous if they like, and space to attend worship without being pressured to join or commit until they are ready to do so.

7. *On the other hand, the leaders in all ministry areas stay focused on the fact that every person who enters our doors is a person for whom Christ died.* We see everyone as a prospect for our church. We may look low-key, but we are evangelistic to the core. We built this place so that people might find new life in Jesus Christ. That is the motivation underneath everything we do. We see every ministry and service offered as a doorway toward opportunities for such an experience with Christ.

The major reason Gulf Breeze Church was able to parlay this thing into a vehicle for reaching so many non-church people is because we were deeply rooted in the mission of hospitality, hope, and healing, outlined in chapter three. We have difficulty imagining ministry that is not grounded in both the felt needs of our community on the one hand and the Great Commission on the other.

It's not just the Community Life Center ministries that work this way. Almost all our ministries are wired this way. Hospitality, hope, and healing are part of the spiritual DNA that has been planted throughout our church. We cannot even build a Habitat house without inviting the owner family to share in the spiritual life of our church. (In fact, two of our Habitat home owners have become church staff members.) Even though we have more than enough kids in our church to fill several good-sized choirs, we cannot offer children's music education on Wednesday afternoon without also marketing to our area public schools and offering school-to-church transportation.

The Community Life Center is able to bridge secular to sacred because it is a ministry of a church that is both able to bridge this gap and committed to doing so. Many churches are now studying this ministry center, expressing an interest in doing something similar in their own communities. This is a wonderful thing. However, these churches will not see comparable results unless they are also on a similar track in terms of their core mission and values.

CHAPTER THREE

Hospitality, Hope, and Healing

At my church, and at yours, most of the things we do, the stories we tell, the songs we sing, the ways we organize, and the principles we teach were passed on to us from others, either from our heritage or from innovative peer congregations. And yet each church is also an original creation, with a mixture of gifts and an apprehension of the good news that is subtly different from any other church in the world. If there is one thing that is unique and perhaps original to Gulf Breeze United Methodist Church, it would be the way in which we frame our mission: "Jesus Christ calls us to reach out with God's love, hospitality, hope, and healing, so that all may experience and share the joy of belonging to Him." We are unaware of any prior instance where the three words *hospitality, hope, and healing* were ever tied together so intentionally. I cannot imagine our church daring to fling open its doors to serve its community and world, were it not for these three values that have sunk deeply into our church's psyche.

In this chapter, I wish to explore what these words mean. I have chosen to use fictional vignettes expressing the actual experiences of people who have come into Gulf Breeze Church. The individuals in these vignettes are composite characters, pulled together from the experiences and testimonies of hundreds of people. My risk in using illustrations so specific to a certain community and culture is that you, the reader, might discount the universal nature of these values. So I ask that you bear with me. Let's experience what these things look like in a particular place first, and then, in chapter eight, we will branch out to consider other ministry contexts.

Hospitality

Jesus created space in his life where strangers could become friends and where persons estranged from God could be reconnected with God. In light of this, it would seem reasonable for churches to be the pacesetters for hospitality in our culture. Reasonable or not, however, most churches do not provide hospitable space for people who live outside of church culture.

> *"Gerri's choir is going to perform at the Methodist Church Sunday morning." Gabe's heart sank. If only it could have been her soccer team. Or a ballet recital. Don't get Gabe wrong. He was glad that Gerri was receiving musical training in an outstanding choral program. He loved the registration fee, which was nothing. But he had hoped that maybe he would get by with simply attending a couple evening concerts a year. Somehow he had not understood up front that her choir would sing occasionally in a regular worship service on Sunday morning. Neither had he contemplated the prospects of having to attend church on those days, dressed formally, and even sitting through a sermon. He was not the kind of guy to whine and complain. But Glenda had been married to Gabe long enough to know that this was a stretch for him. Gabe worked hard six days a week and appreciated the restful pace of Sunday mornings. Sunday was his day.*
>
> *Gabe had never been impressed with organized religion. He wasn't an atheist by any stretch. In fact, he considered himself a believer of sorts. Gabe had been introduced to Christianity as a participant in a vital youth ministry at a military base chapel back when he was in middle school. But he had never figured out churches. The culture of church simply did not make sense to him. It seemed alien to the rest of his life. The image that came to him was Fred Flintstone and Barney Rubble at the Royal Order of Water Buffalos. To Gabe, organized religion was prehistoric, awkwardly formal, often a bit silly, and a terrible drain of money that could be going directly to community needs. The only time Gabe*

went to church was for weddings and an occasional funeral. Gabe possessed no memory of a particularly pleasant visit to a church. Gabe was anything but selfish. He devoted countless hours to youth athletics in the community, coaching teams both for his seventh grade son, Geoff, and his second-grader, Gerri.

"Well I'm sure as hell not wearing a tie," Gabe said quietly to Glenda later that same evening. "Not wearing a tie? You never wear a tie, Gabe." It took a minute for Glenda to tune in to the fact that Gabe was still thinking and debriefing about having to go to church on Sunday.

Four days passed like lightning, the way time passes when a root canal looms ahead. That weekend, Gabe, Glenda, Geoff, and Gerri did something they had never done before. They all piled in the Grand Cherokee and went to church. Gerri was delighted. Geoff was curious. Glenda was cheerfully resigned to sitting through the equivalent of a dry PTA meeting in order to see the show she had come for. As for Gabe, well, he needed an Excedrin.

They arrived by five 'til nine, since Gerri's choir was meeting to rehearse briefly before the 9:30 service. Two blocks away from the church, the first thing they noticed was a police car with red lights flashing near the main parking entrance. "Uh-oh." Gabe said, "Looks like one of the church ladies must have had a fender bender." However, when they got to the scene of the flashing lights, there was no disabled motorist in sight. There were simply cars and pedestrians everywhere. The police officer was directing traffic. "Oh look," cried Geoff from the backseat, "there's Kyle Rogers!" One of Geoff's classmates was walking with a friend across the church lawn. As they drove around looking for a parking spot, Glenda commented, "There are a lot of people here. Half the town is here. I had no idea this place was so big." Upon finding a parking spot, they began to walk back toward the sanctuary, the one that "looked like it must be the main church." Glenda suggested that Gabe and Geoff find a seat while she took Gerri to the music room.

Gabe and Geoff were about to go inside when Geoff spotted a table with bagels under a large white tent on the front lawn. So they stopped and nibbled on bagels. Gabe grabbed a cup of coffee. As he took the first sip, he glanced around under the tent. He saw scores of people, and very few neckties. All ages. Laughing, telling stories. It was like a party. There was even mood music playing, pretty good stuff though he couldn't make out the words. Gabe began to relax a bit.

As he and Geoff approached the main entrance to go inside, they were greeted by three different people with smiles and handshakes and a chipper "Good Morning," each time. Inside, the downstairs was not nearly as full as he expected. Apparently an earlier service had just adjourned. People were busy moving equipment around on the stage. Others were picking up loose papers between the seats and cleaning up the place for the next crowd. There was music playing on the sound system that sounded like Gabe's radio station, but he didn't know the song.

Gabe opened the program he had been handed and was fascinated by the church's calendar of events with certainly more than a hundred different activities scheduled for every age and interest in the upcoming seven days. He noticed that the pastor's topic for the morning was about stress management rather than fire and brimstone. Gabe chuckled to himself, "My image of church is getting stretched here."

Meanwhile, Glenda was walking back from the music room through a brightly-lit corridor as crowded as a mall at Christmas time. She noticed the beautiful wall displays highlighting various activities. The colors and imaginative designs. As a graphic artist, she was impressed with the quality and care that had gone into each display. There was still plenty of time before the service and Gabe had a seat saved for her. So when she passed the bookstore a second time, she stopped to browse. It looked much like the Christian bookstore at the mall. In fact, for a fleeting moment, Glenda felt as if she were actually at the mall. This was not a bad feeling. Glenda loved the mall.

Glenda had been raised Roman Catholic, but stopped attending Mass in her teen years. In her adulthood, she had felt increasingly alienated from the church due to what she perceived as its irrelevancy in its positions on social issues, not to mention its remote practical value to daily life. However, today as she glanced across the assorted titles on display in the bookstore, this place felt anything but irrelevant. "Why are all these people here on a Sunday *morning?" she wondered. "They don't look like it's out of guilt. In fact, they look like they are glad to be here."*

When she arrived in the main room, she saw Geoff waving at her about half way down to the front. By the time she found her seat, she was actually looking forward to the service. She sensed an expectancy in the air similar to what one might find before one of the Broadway series plays that passed through the big theater downtown. Even Gabe seemed to have shed his grumpy mood since last she saw him. "This is okay," she thought.

We live in a customer service era. Churches, for the most part, are not in the lead here. Rather, we find secular organizations and companies like Disney and Wal-Mart are the ones raising the bar for how people expect to be treated. The institutions that will thrive and grow in this new century will increasingly be measured against such rising standards of excellence. The grocery store where people have to wait ten minutes to check out with three items will be history.

And then we come to church. Does anyone meet us as we approach the building with a smile and a cheerful greeting? And is their greeting authentic or does it seem canned? Is the welcome table or information center clearly visible? Is the person at that table winsome? Do they seem to like us? When we ask a question about a location, does someone stop what they are doing and walk with us, like they would at Wal-Mart? Is everything that we see freshly trimmed, planted, weeded, swept, painted, etc.? Are all printed materials that find their way into our hands crisp, attractive, and up to date? Is the music that plays outside and inside creating the kind of ambiance that makes us want to be here and want to come back? Is the sanctuary or worship area appropriately illumined and inviting? Are the seats comfortable? Do people around us look happy? Is laughter heard? Are we welcomed warmly without being singled out, embarrassed, or interviewed? Are we made to feel "a part of the gang"? Does the whole place seem real and down to earth?

Is this a place where people care about us and the things we care about?

The truth of the matter is that we size up most places we visit in the first few minutes of our visit, be it the grocery store, the church, or the computer repair shop. Within just five or ten minutes, we know if we feel good about the place, if it is our kind of place, and whether or not we will likely ever return. The clock starts ticking as soon as we drive on to church property, not when we get inside! By the time the service begins, we have already formed a preliminary judgment.

First impressions last. Forget the sermon and the snazzy choir anthem! Strong opinions are being formed long before these events. The perceived quality of the sermon and the music will, in fact, rest as much on the mood that has been cast with first impressions as by the objective quality of what we say or sing.

"Is this place for me?" That is what we all ask.

What do we do when we encounter greeters whose clothing makes us feel underdressed, or music that sounds to us like it's from another planet, or a confusing worship bulletin that assumes we know the routine and have memorized the creeds? We check out mentally. That is what we do. And at the first available opportunity, we will check out physically, get into our car, and never look back.

Others First

A church, if it is to be a hospitable place, must think about its guests and newcomers more than it thinks about its own tastes and needs. For several years now at Gulf Breeze, we have been unapologetic in saying that we exist first for the people who have never been inside our walls before. Almost all our new members understand this value before they sign on.

No church is a private club, regardless of signals we may send that communicate the contrary. A church, by its God-given nature, belongs to every resident in the community. It is theirs. They may not have a position of leadership; they may have never been to a service or put a dime in the collection, but it is their place. It is important that the community be taught this critical truth. It takes constant effort because we are swimming against the common way that people think about churches. In the United States, churches have been privatized to the point that most folks see churches as organizations that exist for dues-paying members, similar to private schools and country clubs. Again, this is the primary reason our church named its first East Campus building a Community Life Center rather than a Family Life Center. We wanted everyone in our community to understand that this place is for them!

If we want to do business with people spiritually, or in any other way, we must create a comfortable space where they can interact with whatever it is we wish to share with them. We must send them away with positive feelings about their experience with us.

Obviously, if we exist to create a hospitable zone where community people can experience the unconditional love of God, we had better take seriously who lives in the community. Who are its people? How do they live their lives? What radio stations do they listen to? How do they like to dress during their well-earned downtime? What are their common struggles and fears? How much attention or anonymity do they want or need?

One of the most horrifying possible experiences for the seventy-five million Americans who are introverts is the weekly ritual where the pastor, trying to be friendly, says, "Now I want all our visitors to stand! Stand where you are! Don't be bashful!" In most cases, it stops there, but too often, it continues, "Now tell us where you are from." This is often experienced as an embarrassing, humiliating exercise. I am no introvert, but I still do not want a spotlight on me that says I am new, or worse, that I am a VISITOR. I want to blend in! If there is a significant chance that someone will be uncomfortable with such a procedure, why do we do it?

Putting Ourselves in Their Shoes

Let's put ourselves in the shoes of the guests who have gotten up the nerve to walk through those doors for the first time! They want to be comfortable. They want to feel like they belong. They most likely do not want to wear some slightly yellowed old badge with red letters that says VISI-TOR, labeling them like some zoo animal to be observed and greeted.

People don't want to be visitors!!!! They want to belong, to feel a part! If I go to church and am called a visitor, I am being told that this is not my place. "Visitor" is insider/outside language. For this reason, we do not have visitors at our church; we have guests . . . and they are only a guest as long as they feel like one. There should be nothing we do on a Sunday morning that overtly distinguishes between members and non-members. Nothing. People can tell us who they are quietly by means of an attendance register or a registration card. They can tell us as much or as little as they like. If we decide to use nametags, then let's use nametags which all look alike, from the pastor's tag to the tag used by the first-time guest. I often lead worship wearing a disposable nametag that reads simply "Paul."

In each of our worship services, the opening greeting is just that: a greeting. This greeting is made either by one of the pastors or a by another member of the worship team who is gifted in warming up a crowd. The greeting can be one of the most difficult things to do in a service, because the crowd is sometimes a bit cold at that point. The person who greets the crowd should seek to avoid announcements if at all possible. Announcements are rather boring and distract attention from the real reason we are all present, which is to encounter God. Churches have plenty of ways to communicate about critical events without relying on lengthy announcements on the front end of their worship services.

In the greeting time, we welcome our guests, sharing the hope that they will relax and enjoy their time with us. We often use humor to help people relax and warm up to what's about to happen. We remind the group that just after the service there are refreshments outside as well as information and a special gift for guests. At our church's Main Campus, this greeting time is playful but low-key. At our church's East Campus, we have a decidedly non-traditional crowd of churchgoers, so we are sometimes "slightly over the edge" in our greeting style. There, we will sometimes show a humorous video that we have produced, which sets up the service theme. Sometimes we play simple games during the greeting, going out into the congregation looking for "contestants." One week during the greeting time, I looked through the crowd for volunteers to cast all the cameo roles for the drama that came later in the service. On one Superbowl Sunday, we played Superbowl Trivia, with one of our band members throwing plastic footballs into the crowd as prizes. A few weeks later, during Mardi Gras, we threw Moon Pies. Obviously, we would never throw Moon Pies in worship in more traditional services. The effect of such playfulness on the front end of worship is to help people relax and open up to experience the worship event that will follow.

One of the ways we can help people feel welcome and comfortable in worship is by addressing them in their own language. Until 1963, the majority of Christian worshipers in the world experienced Mass in Latin. This essentially meant that the leaders cared more about traditional language than about communicating the faith. This practice of Latin-only in church went on about a thousand years too long. It said to the average worshiper that the church did not care to speak to them. That is the very opposite of hospitality.

Forty years after Vatican II eliminated the Latin-only rule, the Roman Catholics are speaking English in North America. But many Protestants are still talking about narthexes, introits, vestries, acolytes, benedictions, and the Eucharist. Still others are talking about "being washed in the blood," "coming before the throne of grace," "Salvation," "Sanctification," etc. This is not to mention all the acronyms and code words that various denominational cultures devise for communication between insiders. The problem with all of the above is that when we use such language, we are talking only to insiders, to people who already understand a specialized language. To everyone else, we might as well be speaking Latin. To the vast majority of people, who don't understand our insider language, we are saying (1) you are an outsider, and (2) we don't care enough about you to communicate with you.

We should, therefore, always carefully think through everything we print and say in public. We are wise to assume no prior theological knowledge or church culture knowledge on the part of the people we are addressing. Despite our best attempts, we will all sometimes let insider language slip through. This has to be an issue of constant self-reflection and vigilance.

A Place for Building Community

Most of the hospitality ministry happens just outside of worship, on the way in, on the way out, and in the hours that follow worship. Several years ago on a financial commitment Sunday, we rented a big tent for the front church lawn for festive music, finger foods, and socializing between services. As people walked toward the sanctuary, they heard Dixieland music and saw other people laughing and having a good time. It made a measurable difference that day when they got inside.

Back at that time, our attendance registration pads that were passed down each row at the start of each service contained a small box, which one could check, which read "Wish to join the church." Typically, one or two persons would check the box any given week. But on this week—the week that all the happy people were outside between the parking area and the sanctuary—twelve persons checked the box. This, on the one week of the year the church asks for money!

So later that year we bought ourselves a tent, not a circus tent, but a tasteful, simple white tent, with open sides that flow into a landscaped plaza and courtyard area. Between one and two hundred people will congregate in the tent area during each break between our Main Campus services. We cannot possibly fit all these people under the tent, so we designed the area for them to spill over in every direction onto the grass and adjacent sidewalk areas. Our weather is such that this arrangement works on all but half a dozen Sundays a year. In the tent area, one will find the hospitality booth and an array of simple refreshments and ministry exhibits. About once a month, something out of the ordinary happens out there. One week we had a four-hour blitz build of a playhouse by our Habitat for Humanity workers to raise awareness about the beginning of another church-sponsored Habitat house. Another week, we had a street musician from the New Orleans French Quarter playing a trumpet. Still another week, there might be bagpipes for St. Patrick's Day. One week we collected hundreds of bottles of Pepto-Bismol to send with a medical mission team to Honduras. That day, the whole tent area was decorated in pink, with a few flamingos in the yard for the crowning touch. The goal each Sunday is a festive, winsome area for human connection after worship.

People drive down the street on the way to the golf course, to Sunday brunch, or to other churches, and they slow down as they pass our Main Campus due to the congested traffic. They almost veer off the street, craning sideways, trying to figure out what, exactly, the Methodists are doing this week. Taking all this festivity outside broadcasts to the whole community that Gulf Breeze Church is a joyful, lively place.

At our East Campus, we do not have a tent, but we do make use of a bright, airy lobby and free space inside the worship area. We do not fill the entire worship space with chairs. We try to leave good mingling room around the back of the room and on the sides. In addition, we have a couple dozen round tables and chairs that run around behind the rows of chairs. We have found that some people are more comfortable worshiping at a round table, in sight of other people, with a beverage in hand.

Greeting Our Guests Like VIPs

On both campuses of our church, we believe that greeters are engaged in one of the most critical of all ministries. It is our goal that everyone is offered three smiles and three handshakes before they are seated in a worship service.

In the book *Inside the Magic Kingdom: Seven Keys to Disney's Success* (Bard Press: Austin, 1997), author Tom Connellan sets forth five standards for how Disney *cast members* (they do not have employees) interact with *guests* (they do not have visitors, either). They are:

1. Always make eye contact and smile.
2. Greet and welcome every guest.
3. Always give outstanding quality service.
4. Exceed guest expectations and seek out guest contacts (i.e., go out of your way to do numbers 1-3).
5. Maintain a personal standard of quality in all you do.

The above is a good start! Disney can take us only so far, but they do suggest a starting line for us. It is Jesus who moves us beyond this minimum standard to the place where the welcome we offer is authentic and from the heart. Jesus models for us the standard of authentic caring for the precious lives of people. Ultimately, most people do not need plastic smiles or happy pretense. There is already enough of that in their lives. Church members are not cast members playing a role. We play ourselves. Christian hospitality has to come from the heart. Christian hospitality continues after hours, when the church's lights are off and the doors are locked, as relationships continue.

For any who might be thinking otherwise, I want to just say right here that this commitment to a warm welcome is not just a strategy or tactic for reaching young adults. The need for positive interaction with winsome human beings is something that transcends generations. All of us appreciate meeting people who are authentically glad to see us and who are interested in who we are. This most basic hospitality may look different in each context, but it is a universal need in every Christian gathering, all the way back to the book of Acts.

The leaders that we deploy into welcoming ministries should be people who truly care about people, who have a desire to see people meet the Lord. When a pastor goes to a declining, in-grown church and wants to turn it around, one of his or her first priorities should be to find people who care about seeing people meet the Lord, and who are comfortable with the diversity of people who need to walk through the church's doors and into its ministries.

Early in a church turn around, a pastor may look across a congregation and find only a few people who fit into this category. Mobilizing this small band to begin to create a zone of caring is one of the first steps necessary in changing the climate of a church. If the ushers are not in sync with the new vision, then we can work around them, creating teams of greeters that get to people before the ushers do and another team that follows up with people to begin establishing relationship.

I consulted with one church who had put a welcoming ministry into place that was well-intentioned but too assertive. They were attempting to pick out new faces on the church sidewalk and in the lobby and to pray with these people before they got fully in the door and found a seat. This behavior was driving more than a few people away from that church. Their heart was in the right place. They failed, however, to provide a comfortable space for the people they wanted to reach.

Deeper than Disney

In 1975, the same year that Herb Sadler was first appointed as pastor at Gulf Breeze United Methodist Church, a classic work on Christian spirituality was published by Henri Nouwen. Years before Herb and I ever met one another, this book became a significant influence on each of us. It was entitled simply *Reaching Out*. I discovered *Reaching Out* about five years after it was published, when I raided a give-away table of unwanted books in the hallway of the religion department at Baylor University. I grabbed an armload of books. Most turned out to be losers. I remember throwing the little stack of books on my bed, flipping through them. I recall picking up *Reaching Out* and opening it, assuming that it, too, was worth about the price I had paid for it. But I didn't set it down until I had finished reading it several hours later. In the midst of the garbage, I had stumbled on to a spiritual treasure.

Reaching Out is divided into three sections, each of which deal with a different aspect, or "movement," of the spiritual life. The middle section of the book made the greatest impact on me. This section is entitled "The Second Movement: From Hostility to Hospitality." Nouwen writes:

> Our society seems to be increasingly full of fearful, defensive, aggressive people anxiously clinging to their property and inclined to look at the surrounding world with suspicion, always expecting an enemy to suddenly appear, intrude and do harm. But . . . our vocation [is] to convert the *hostis* into a *hospes*, the enemy into a guest and to create the free and fearless space where brotherhood and sisterhood can be formed and fully experienced. (p. 46)

Hospitality . . . means primarily the creation of a free
space where the stranger can enter and become a friend
instead of an enemy. Hospitality is not to change people, but
to offer them a space where change can take place. (p. 51)

We cannot force anyone to such an intimate change of
heart, but we can offer the space where such change can
take place. (p. 54)

I first read the above words in the context of my experience as a college sophomore, disturbed by the extremely
aggressive and hostile forms of evangelism that were being
modeled by students on my campus. Another twenty years
and a series of evangelism awards have come and gone in
my life since that time. I had almost forgotten how uncomfortable I used to be with aggressive "witnessing," until just
recently. A friend and I were eating lunch at a Wendy's
restaurant across from two women who were literally
accosting a third woman with "the plan of Salvation" as
they understood it. We didn't know whether to ignore it,
intervene in their private conversation, or call 9-1-1! It was
a scary thing to watch! Nouwen put into eloquent words
what I had been feeling since I was fourteen years old: it
just isn't right to attack a person with our religion, even if
we are trying to help them.

But when Nouwen offered us his insights on hospitality,
it was not with fundamentalism in mind; he was thinking
about something very different. He writes:

As a reaction to a very aggressive, manipulative and
often degrading type of evangelization, we sometimes
have become hesitant to make our own religious convictions known, thereby losing our sense of witness . . . .
it belongs to the core of Christian spirituality to reach out
to each other with good news and to speak without
embarrassment about what we "have heard and . . .
seen with our own eyes . . . watched and touched with
our own hands" (1 John 1:1).

It isn't belligerent evangelism that afflicts most churches. It is the lack of evangelism altogether. This hesitation to offer our witness is the main reason that church-based community centers failed in the '70s. Offering social services and recreation is not enough.

Christian hospitality is far more than simply basketball for community teens or cookies and punch after church. Christian hospitality should always be purposeful. And the purpose should be to create space for transformation, both of ourselves and of the stranger.

Letting the Spirit Work the Magic

Effective evangelism is not about a formula. Evangelism is rooted in authentic relationships and empowered by the Holy Spirit. Because so many have joined our church by
· profession of their faith, other church leaders occasionally ask for the text of our guest-response form letters, as if to suggest that there is some special wording there. I try to tell those folks to forget about our form letters. There is nothing special there. There is nothing particularly notable or profound about any of our follow-up procedures. We try to stay in touch with people without hounding them. So do a lot of other churches. Effective evangelism is not about a magic method or formula. It *is* strongly connected, however, to a climate of hospitality which we have worked hard to establish and maintain.

Ultimately, hospitality is the work of the Holy Spirit. This is seen so clearly in Acts 2, as the Spirit descended in power upon the early church, leading the believers into the streets where they spoke the good news in terms that all could understand and receive. It is God, who bonds us all together, not evangelism procedures.

Some villages, such as Chicago, have very tall buildings that funnel the wind down certain streets, magnifying the wind velocity. We call this effect a "wind tunnel." When we create hospitality procedures, it is akin to building tall buildings that can catch God's wind as it blows through our community. However, without the God factor, all the great designs and plans we can think of are of little effect.

Every community is different in terms of people's expectations of and receptivity to a church's hospitality. When other church leaders visit Gulf Breeze, the last thing we would desire would be for them to go home and simply duplicate our hospitality systems and practices. The systems and practices vary even between our two campuses. Rather, we would hope they would leave challenged to look at the people in their communities and design systems of hospitality that are indigenous and natural to each setting. And most important, we would hope that they would leave trusting the Holy Spirit to work the magic of Pentecost.

Hope

God's hospitality is not an end in itself. God is not interested simply in giving us warm fuzzies. We each receive the warm embrace of God so that we might be changed. And the change comes as God is able to interject hope into our lives.

Our team of pastors has a rather simple goal in every sermon we preach, in every service we lead. Our larger team of leaders extends this goal to every activity we plan. The goal is to see that people experience Good News. We want to send them home with HOPE!

Dave still becomes physically ill just thinking about the night he was arrested for drunk driving. He had worked so hard to gain custody of his two sons. He had put his needs behind the needs of his kids for so many years that he didn't know any other way to think. And yet, every other weekend, when the boys would go to visit their mother, Dave would always try to have a little "fun for Dave." One Saturday night he joined a couple of work buddies watching game two of the World Series. He knew as he backed out the friend's driveway to go home, he should have stopped and gone back inside. But he didn't stop.

As he rode to the police station, the tears fell freely down his face. He sat in the dark rear of the police car, thinking about his boys, certain that he would lose custody of his children because of this.

Because it was a first offense, Dave was given a probated sentence, a stiff fine, and was required to do 40 hours of community service. One of his choices of community service was to work at the new community center run by Gulf Breeze United Methodist Church. He made an appointment with Anita Sharron, the overseer of the community service ministry. He mildly dreaded the appointment, having not been to a church in at least a decade. But, to his surprise, Anita did not care about his past or about his crime. She seemed to take an immediate liking to him, telling him that he would work on Saturday evenings and Sunday mornings. For a couple of hours on Saturdays, he was to help set up the gym for Sunday worship, moving chairs and tables. Sunday mornings he was to work with the building superintendent for another three hours. He could work off his time in just a few weekends. When the boys were home, they could come with him. She told him to dress casual for Sunday.

He chose, for his first community service weekend, a week when the boys were with their mother. He arrived on Sunday a bit apprehensive, but resigned to the fact that he would live through it, and thankful for the fact that he was being given a second chance. As he walked into the building, he heard a band playing, and saw the early crew of volunteers laughing and enjoying each other's company. Anita came across the lobby to welcome him and then to introduce him to the others, none of whom had any idea why he was at church that morning. Suddenly, he realized that he was being treated as if he were just a guy in town who had come to volunteer at church. He helped with a couple of set-up tasks and began to warm up to one of the greeters who was talking about his fishing expedition the day before.

Then the service started. At this point, Dave's job was to sit toward the back, watch the door for latecomers, and to put out extra chairs as they were needed. He immediately found himself truly enjoying the music, then engaged in the message, which included a clip from one of his favorite movies. The message was on new beginnings, of all things. Dave thought to himself, "If I had known there was a church like this, I would have been here all along, every week."

As he left, he saw a group of middle-schoolers skateboarding in one section of the parking lot. A middle-aged woman saw the direction he was looking and said, "The skateboarding Sunday school class. I wish they'd had something like that when I was that age." Dave immediately thought of his oldest son, Brandon. And then he delighted in the fact that he would be able to share this place with Brandon the following week. He would have Brandon bring his skateboard along.

Dave completed his eight weeks and never stopped coming to set up chairs. He became a greeter. His boys got involved in youth ministry. He joined a single parents group after the worship service. And then one Sunday, the pastor invited folks to give their lives to Christ totally, and he did so. In the darkened room where the service was held, he felt the privacy to shed tears as he prayed. It was the first time he had cried since his ride in the police car. He thanked God for second chances. Soon after, he became a member of the church.

What Dave did not realize was that there were about two dozen other Daves in the room with him at that very moment, each of whom had first come to work off their community service hours.

Since its 1995 renovation, the Main Campus sanctuary at Gulf Breeze has had an interior visual focal point that is, so far as we are aware, the only one of its kind in the world. This focal point is a large, rugged metal cross suspended behind the choir area with a skylight in a large shaft directly above it. Beneath the skylight, hidden from the congregation's view is a 1,200 pound prism of solid glass, which catches the sun's rays and translates them into a dazzling rainbow that splashes over the cross. The movement of the sun and clouds causes the rainbow to expand and contract constantly, creating a slow-motion light show that extends throughout a morning worship service. This rainbow over the cross makes a dramatic statement about resurrection, joy, and hope. In just a few years, this cross and rainbow has become the central visual insignia of our ministry. We think, and would hope that you agree, that this is a more fitting and comprehensive symbol of our faith than simply a cross.

Let's be honest: church can be a pretty depressing place. It can be so stuffy and out of touch. Or it can be obsessed with Washington politics and messy social issues that leave us feeling angry and overwhelmed. Or it can turn into an all-out attack on the worshipers themselves for their many personal shortfalls. I visit with lots of folks who are returning to church after many years away. One of the leading reasons they share for having dropped out of church is their experience of feeling constantly attacked from the pulpit. Millions of people go to church each Sunday looking for hope, only to be depressed by what is done and said.

People are better motivated when we call them to something higher, when we offer them a positive vision. When we constantly cast a positive, hopeful vision, we attract positive, hopeful people into leadership. When we constantly dwell on "how dire everything is," either at the church, in Washington, or in society at large, we attract negative, fearful people into leadership.

Herb Sadler is fond of saying, "People get beat up by life six days a week. They don't need to get beat up at church." People need to find strength, encouragement, and hope. They need to have their vision lifted—not to come away understanding the problem better, but to see a way through. Every message and worship service is designed to be hope-filled and encouraging, even as we sometimes deal with painful subjects. People come to church with painful awareness that something is wrong in their lives and in the world. Our job is not to rub their faces in what is wrong, or to throw their sins at them. Our job is to throw grace at them!

In our orientation class we often ask participants two questions: (1) "Why did you come here the first time?" and

(2) "Why did you come back?" Their answer to the first question tells us what our reputation is. Their answer to the next question tells us something about how effective we are. Invariably, they talk about the positive, hopeful approach at our church. Hope is the major, central theme of our church's ministry.

Let's look at three ways that we can all intentionally nurture an atmosphere of hope. These three ways are through preaching, through church financial management, and through the celebration of things that unite us together.

Hope in Preaching and Teaching

A message on Sunday (or the teaching in a class or small group) is hopeful to me if I can understand it, can relate it clearly to my life challenges, and can walk away with tools to more effectively deal with those challenges. The same message will be hopeless to me if I can't understand it, can't clearly relate it to the burning issues of my life, or I walk away overwhelmed, confused, or no more equipped to deal with those issues than I was before.

Hope-filled preaching and teaching

1. deals with life issues of interest to ordinary people,
2. uses words and concepts that unchurched people can understand,
3. uses story and contemporary illustration to make the point(s),
4. proclaims a strong sense of "Thus says the Lord,"
5. uses warm humor (as opposed to sarcasm),
6. paints a picture of the positive possibilities for our lives,
7. unfolds the truth of Scripture plainly,
8. offers people life-sized bites (as opposed to throwing global issues at them that are bigger than they can respond to),
9. invites people to concrete behaviors and responses,
10. maintains strong eye contact between preacher and listeners.

Here are traits that work against hope. The presence of even one of these can be a major communication handicap. Two or more can be deadly.
Preaching and teaching that works against hope

1. deals at length with insider issues, exegetical issues, or theological issues not of immediate interest to the average listener,
2. uses insider language without explanation,
3. has too much theory with too little concrete illustration or no story,
4. communicates a sense of "maybe" or "not sure," perhaps focusing on historical/critical reading of Scripture at the expense of the text's message,
5. is either without humor or the humor is mean-spirited,
6. focuses on how bad we are,
7. is not clearly related to the Scripture, which may have been read without explanation several minutes prior to the actual message,
8. focuses on issues that are overwhelming or politically complex,
9. stops short of offering practical help for daily living,
10. is read from a manuscript.

There are many pastors, honestly puzzled by their church's lack of growth, whose preaching is largely described by the latter list. They may be preaching the way they were taught. Or they may have never received coaching in effective public speaking. These pastors may be trying to turn around declining congregations, unwittingly working against themselves with their preaching. "Hopeless" preaching can be a major inhibitor of growth in a church. We pastors can become the problem even as we look for solutions.

Christian communicators are servants of good news. Whatever models and mentors we use, the prophet Amos probably should *not* be our primary model. Nor should anyone who sounds like him. Amos was angry with the people to whom he was preaching. There is seldom a place for such anger in Christian proclamation. We don't need cranky, cantankerous leaders sharing the good news!! Passion, yes. Indignation, occasionally. Compassion and hope, always. Hostility, never.

Angry preaching does not help to build the kind of spiritual village I am describing here. The greatest giver of hope in my lifetime thus far has been Martin Luther King, Jr. The most notable thing about his preaching is that it was passionate and hopeful. It was seldom, if ever, angry preaching. He never forgot that he was a servant of good news.

Sarcasm is language that taunts another, usually in the form of humor. It arises from anger, and is very common in everyday life. We hear sarcasm on talk radio. We hear it at work. The usual result is that people laugh at other people. When sarcasm is about people, it can run dangerously close to what Jesus warned us about in Matthew 5, when he told us not to call our brother a fool. There is no place for sarcasm in Christian preaching. There is no case in the New Testament where Jesus or any apostle used sarcasm in the sharing of the good news. When we hear sarcastic remarks directed at us, people like us, or people we respect, we become defensive. The doors of communication slam shut.

As a very young pastor, I once used sarcasm in a sermon, taking an indirect jab at a group of people who had been unhappy about the relocation of the church nursery. After that sermon, this group of people felt even more angry and misunderstood than when it had been a simple disagreement. Such sarcasm in the pulpit can quickly poison the spirit of a church. It tears apart the community. It diminishes hope.

One of the most hopeful things that can happen in the preaching event is for a listener to conclude, "This pastor understands me. This pastor is talking to me. This pastor cares about me." I am convinced there is no better way to communicate this sense than in looking at people as we talk to them.

When we started our first worship service at the East Campus, I stopped using a pulpit or podium. I kept a barstool center stage where I could sit. Some weeks, I would just stand and talk, setting my Bible on the barstool except when I was reading from it. Operating like this, obviously there were often things I intended to say that I forgot to say. However the only ones who know I am lost are God, me, and the people running audio/visuals, who have a rough manuscript in hand.

For whatever is lost from the message for lack of notes, much more is gained in the perception that "Paul is right there with us, talking to us, chatting with us, as if he were sitting in our living room." People remember more about *how* we say something than *what* we say. Of what we actually say, they are most likely to remember humorous anecdotes and stories. They also remember personal references, what we tell them about our own experience, about what is happening or has happened in our own lives.

Standing up to speak without a pulpit or a manuscript can be a bit scary at first. But this also says some very positive things to people. It says that I care about them more than I care about my notes. It says that the message is really about them and their concerns. It says that this is a live event, a live conversation, not a reading of something that was decided and scripted at an earlier time. These are each very hopeful things.

Wooden boxes and pages of notes can become barriers between people. Flinging open the doors means we need to rethink the ways we communicate the good news, so that we might eliminate or minimize these barriers.

Hope in Financial Management

Hope must permeate a congregation's culture. Controlling, defensive, financial management can be just as debilitating to a congregation's health as negative, angry preaching. Changing the tone of the preaching often involves a simple decision process within one person (the pastor). Changing the tone of the financial management is often a more complicated proposition, involving numerous congregational leaders. But it is equally important!

Not long after I finished seminary, I was sent to serve as pastor of a church that had some financial problems. On my first Sunday there, the call to worship was offered by one of the church's leaders who announced to the congregation that the church did not have enough money that week to pay the mortgage or the preacher. The community in which the church was located was mired in a terrible recession. Our house in that town was surrounded by vacant houses in various states of disrepair. Businesses were hurting due to the population drop as families left looking for work elsewhere. The church's proper role was to be a bastion of hope in the midst of this community crisis. Imagine how people felt when they entered what they had hoped was a sanctuary from their overdue bills and other life stresses, only to be greeted by the word that the church was in financial crisis. Some of them undoubtedly felt betrayed by their church, for it to be broadcasting despair rather than hope. It should have been no wonder that attendance dropped steadily in the weeks that followed. A few were motivated to give more money. More than a few were motivated to go fishing.

When Herb Sadler arrived as pastor at Gulf Breeze, the church was budgeted well beyond its income, with leaders who were obsessed with the lack of money. One of the first things he led the church to do that year was to build a budget that was one hundred percent underwritten by pledges, and then live with it. This meant a sharp budget cut initially. But this action moved the finances into the black and took away the biggest weapon that the negative, controlling leaders had. Since that time, the church has typically focused on money only two Sundays out of the year.

After two weeks of teaching on stewardship and tithing, a church can gather pledges from its people and build a budget for the following year based upon pledges received. Because the budget is built by the faith of the people, as demonstrated by their pledges, that church will not have to focus on money again in worship for fifty weeks. Throughout the year, as new members are received, they can be challenged to tithe or begin stepping toward tithing. In those occasional years when a church chooses to run a capital fund campaign to finance new construction, the stewardship focus can be extended to five or six weeks.

We know that too much talk about money is one of the most often reasons cited by people who hate going to church as to why they hate going to church. On the other hand, it is amazing how a church's negative attitude can turn around once its financial problems are diffused. Many churches are constantly trying to stretch themselves in terms of staff and program and facilities. But stretching to the point of over-budgeting can become counter-productive. If a church is constantly behind its budget in its giving, that church may be constantly teaching itself that it is a failure.

On the other hand, living within our means fuels and supports a positive and hopeful atmosphere. The contribution of such an atmosphere to a church's life is worth far more than any of the things a church loses when they decide to limit their spending plan to their income. This is a truth that many church leaders have yet to grasp.

In the simplest of terms, we are in the good news business. No matter what financial challenges are before us, we must always frame those challenges with a spirit of hope.

Hope in the Celebration of Things That Unite

We must choose to find common ground in our belief that Jesus is Lord, and to celebrate that common ground, while allowing some diversity of belief around the table.

There is little value in dwelling on the ways we differ. Spotlighting diversity may be interesting from a sociological perspective, but it does not rally us together. We spotlight the common ground that unites us in diversity. We believe that is a strategy with roots all the way back to the book of Acts.

Can anyone imagine church officials in the first century asking each congregation for a report on what percentage of their people were Jew and what percentage were Gentile? Peter and Paul would be aghast at the idea. If the point of the church were representation of diversity, it might make sense to keep tabs on such things. But representation of diversity is not the point of the church. The point of the church is to unite diverse people in a common mission. And in that mission, there were probably some questions best not asked, and some statistics best not kept, in first century church life. Circumcision being among them. Better that we find the common ground and celebrate that!

We should celebrate great ministry! This celebration takes many forms, including inviting members of mission teams to share about their work, interviewing leaders or beneficiaries of various ministries, and inviting participants in our youth ministry to lead our worship services regularly. In each case, people are left feeling good about their church and the difference it is making in people's lives.

We see the pastor's column of our weekly newsletter as an opportunity to cheer on the incredible things that our people are doing in ministry. We can celebrate ministry successes in our sermon illustrations. We can constantly look for ways and places to share the good news of what God is doing among us.

Each year on the Sunday before our people make their commitments to participation and leadership in particular ministries for the coming year, we hold a Ministry Fair on both campuses of our church. The Ministry Fair is an opportunity for each ministry team in the church to create an information booth to share the story of what they are doing, and to invite others to join them. That Sunday is one of the most energy-filled days of the year. People see numerous tables and ministries all under the umbrella of their church, and they feel good. Hope is everywhere on Ministry Fair Day.

Herb Sadler began telling a small church in Gulf Breeze how great they were back in days when a lot of folks in the church were still mired in negativity and inward thinking. There was nothing dishonest here. Looking past the negative behaviors, every time he would see someone getting the right idea and doing the right thing, he would celebrate it. If you keep telling someone what a good job they are doing, pretty soon, they will be doing a better job still!

When there is controversy, we run for the common ground and set up our stakes to homestead there. There is almost always a controversy brewing in most Christian denominations, and in most local communities. We could spend all our energy fighting all kinds of battles on every front. At Gulf Breeze, we choose to sit out most of those fights, unless we perceive that the very essence and integrity of our congregation's ministry is at stake, or there is a wider crisis to which we must speak a word of perspective and hope.

Running for the common ground is not the same as fence-sitting. It is not based upon the lack of convictions. Rather, it is based upon discerning the deepest Christian convictions that transcend the partisan and emotional issues that come and go in human life.

When an abortion doctor was shot and killed in our city a few years ago, we found common ground in our belief that human life is a sacred thing and that abortion is a tragic thing. We could agree furthermore that the best way to change society is through non-violent means. The majority of our congregation abhors abortion, but we are diverse in our beliefs about the role of the law in moral issues involving a woman's body. There is no way that our church could reach consensus on the *political* questions of "right to life" versus "right to choose" without simply splitting ourselves into two churches. Perhaps some churches can find such consensus; we cannot. We feel that the resulting turmoil would only weaken our influence for good and derail what God is seeking to do through us.

Fortunately, the majority of our members vote their conscience and speak freely about their convictions. They also respect one another, and have experienced the reality that persons of devout belief sometimes reach different conclusions on this and other political questions. And they choose to be a church together despite such differences. We find the common ground! And we celebrate it.

In recent years, church music has been used often as a rallying issue to divide churches. At Gulf Breeze, though our music is decidedly diverse between our five Sunday services, it remains the single greatest rallying point of our unity. Music transcends most of the ideologies that have historically divided Christians. The profound experience of unity through the act of praise and worship marks almost every regional church that I know. There are probably few churches in North America more diverse than the Brooklyn Tabernacle in New York City. There are also few churches where spirit-driven music more profoundly enables people to transcend their personal agendas and to be united in something bigger than themselves. Great music that touches the hearts of people and draws them toward the love and worship of God is an essential part of a church's life.

It is sadly ironic that some churches fight over the very thing that holds such promise to draw their people together. In the choice to resist a broader and more heartfelt range of music in worship, we Christians often shoot ourselves in both feet.

Healing

I will never forget an interview between John Wimber and Peter Jennings that aired several years ago on ABC television. John Wimber is the founder of the Vineyard movement, a network of charismatic congregations. John describes reading the Gospels and the book of Acts as a young Christian and then going to a mainline church, listening to a sermon and thinking to himself, "This is all nice, but when do they *do it?* When do they do the stuff?" So he asked the pastor as he went out the door, "So when do you do the stuff?" The pastor replied with a puzzled look, "What stuff?" "You know, *the stuff,* the stuff Jesus did, when do the lame get to walk? When do the blind get their sight?"

Wimber was raising a very good question. We follow Jesus. Jesus was a healer. So when do we get around to "the stuff" Jesus did? Most churches do not have a compelling answer to this question: Do we believe in healing?

The events of the last week of August 1999 are almost surreal to Janet as she tries to reconstruct them. She knew her marriage to Bart was a bit stressed at times, but they were both busy in their careers, she had just been promoted at work, and she considered herself happy. She thought Bart was happy. Their kids were doing well in school and staying out of trouble. Bart had his idiosyncrasies, but she had made peace with those years ago. And then, without warning, there came the day when he told her that he did not love her anymore, and he loved another, and that he was leaving. Within seventy-two hours, almost every article and object related to Bart had been moved out of the house. She kept thinking it would have been easier if Bart had been hit by a truck. At least then she would not feel the shame and the rejection.

When Janet returned to work, as a floor manager at a large department store, everyone in the store seemed to know what had happened. It seemed to Janet that they were all looking at her with pity in their eyes, and this filled her with anger. That evening, after work, she sat in a Mexican restaurant for three solid hours, drowning her sorrows in Diet Pepsi. Bart had the kids tonight and she dreaded returning to an empty house on a Saturday evening.

Finally, she left for home. As she crossed the three-mile bridge from Pensacola to Gulf Breeze, where she lived, her speed surpassed 65 miles-per-hour in a 45 mile-per-hour zone. When she entered Gulf Breeze city limits, the speed limit dropped to 35.

Janet's speed did not. Within seconds, red lights were flashing in the rearview mirror. Soon, a wiry woman in a police uniform was standing at the window of Janet's car. The name on her badge read "Garvey."

Officer Garvey asked Janet, "Ma'am, did you realize you were going 63 miles-per-hour in a 35 mile-per-hour zone?" Janet replied that she had no idea how fast she was going. At this particular moment, she really didn't care how fast she was going, but stopped short of saying so. The officer noticed the smeared mascara and realized that Janet had been crying. After she issued the citation, she said, "You seem quite upset. Are you okay?" Janet said, "Other than the fact that my husband just left me, I am perfectly fine."

What happened in the next fifteen minutes was one of the more unusual conversations between a ticketing officer and a motorist in the history of our community. Officer Garvey looked at Janet with a mischievous smile and said, "Can I ask you something personal?" Janet said, "Sure." "Do you go to church anywhere?" Janet was surprised by the officer's question. She paused a moment and then replied that she and her husband were relatively new to town and that they had not found a church. She had, in fact, lived in the community for six years now. The officer said, "When I went through my divorce three years ago, it was Gulf Breeze United Methodist Church who stood with me and helped me through it. It's just up the road about two blocks and then you take a right at the light, another block and you are there. I hope you will try it."

Thirty-six hours later, Janet showed up for church. Greeting people at one of the side doors was a familiar face, the face of Linda Garvey, except this time, she wasn't in uniform. Linda and Janet sat together in church. Linda passed Janet a brochure about the upcoming Divorce Recovery class, the same program that Linda had found so helpful three years earlier. The class would meet over nine consecutive Monday nights. After the service was over, Janet decided to sign up for Divorce Recovery. Her divorce was still several weeks away, but she was ready to begin healing.

On the first night of Divorce Recovery, Janet arrived to find twenty-five other people of all ages, seventeen women and eight men, led by a team of four persons; a professional counselor and three table leaders, each of whom had gone through the divorce recovery process themselves. The session was upbeat, and the sharing was made easy and natural. For the next nine weeks, Monday nights were the high point of Janet's week.

By the end of the nine weeks, Janet transitioned into a Sunday morning small group of single women with high school children.

A few months later, when Janet decided to join the church, it was explained to her that joining meant "moving from the bleachers to the playing field." Joining means becoming a partner in ministry and finding a place of service. Janet called the leader of her Divorce Recovery class and asked if she could train to be a table leader in the next class. Janet had, in seven months, come full circle, from a person in need of God's healing to a person ready to share that healing with others.

Healing was at the heart of Jesus' ministry, as central to what he was about as was his teaching. In fact, it is really difficult to separate the two. Each was a natural extension of the other. He taught about God's love and he was a conduit for that love. Across the years, Jesus' disciples have been quite comfortable with the teaching end of ministry. But a lot of us have grown quite uncomfortable and awkward with the healing end. There are several reasons for this discomfort with healing.

One reason is our reaction to and distaste for healing services that resemble a circus sideshow. I share this concern about sensationalism in healing ministries. A woman called me one time to ask, "What do you think about Benny Hinn?" I replied, "I try not to think about Benny Hinn." Many folks allow the Benny Hinns of the world to define for us what Christian healing means. To go back to John Wimber's language, I am often uncomfortable with the way some churches try to do "the stuff."

Another reason we are sometimes uncomfortable with healing is that we are afraid that nothing will happen even after we earnestly pray for something to happen. We are afraid that we will raise false hopes in the case of a terminal illness, or that we will look like fools by praying fervently for something that never happens.

Still another reason that some Christians are uncomfortable with this is because they have been taught that miracles ceased with the death of the apostles. That is a highly dubious proposition. I can find no biblical basis for it, yet it has enjoyed wide circulation.

In Romans 8:28, Paul writes, "We know that all things work together for good for those who love God, who are called according to his purpose." God can take even bad things, broken situations that sadden him, and use those things for his purposes. Another way of putting it is this: God can always do something beautiful with the broken pieces of our lives, if we give all those pieces to him in faith. This hope-filled idea is the basis for a positive emphasis on healing.

When Do We Do the Stuff?

In the book of James, Christians are taught that when they are sick they should call for the elders of the church to pray over them and anoint them with oil so that they might be made well. Several years ago, the leadership of our church decided that we needed to take seriously this important facet of our appointed work as Christ's representatives in the world.

One result of this decision is that today our church offers three opportunities for prayers for healing each Sunday morning. Hundreds have participated in these services over the years; about half coming with a personal need for healing. The others come on behalf of a loved one. A pastor or one of our lay pastors lays hands on the head of the person coming with a request for healing. Often we make the sign of the cross on the forehead before we lay hands on their head for prayer. Many remarkable stories of God's goodness and gracious healing have stemmed from this ministry. There is nothing flamboyant or eccentric about this ministry.

We pray for physical healing, for emotional healing, for spiritual healing, for relational healing, for healing of memories. Wherever we experience brokenness, we reach out to God and ask for his healing touch.

This emphasis on healing is what has given teeth and integrity to the mission of our church. Hospitality and hope are nice. But it is our belief that God transforms brokenness and redeems lives, enabling people to walk, through hope, into new life.

We approach the subject with humility. It isn't as if those of us who offer the healing of Christ are totally healed ourselves. Healing is a process that lasts beyond a lifetime. We talk often about our church being a hospital where Christ is the physician and the rest of us are patients. Herb Sadler will tell you, "I'm not even a nurse here. I'm just a patient sharing with other patients what I have experienced and what has been helpful." Everyone who has ever walked through our doors in the past is broken, somehow or another. And the same is true of everyone who will walk through our doors next week. Some of us are recovering. Others of us are just beginning. But our belief that we all need healing keeps us from getting into an "us versus them" mentality of saved and unsaved.

This gives people freedom and permission to be themselves in our midst—permission to not be perfect. No one has to pretend to have it all together when they don't. This is especially important for people who are new to church life. There have been those who look at the motley crew we have gathered at our church and conclude that we are not holy enough or spiritual enough. But with our lack of pretense, it will always be a stretch to call us hypocrites.

In our preaching, each of the pastors, when we tell stories on ourselves, look for stories that show our humanity. We will tell stories in which we can laugh at ourselves, or demonstrate our failures or ineptitude in some situation. This is disarming for people, giving them permission to enter where they are.

Healing Is for Leaders, Too

In the spring of 2000, my wife and I sent a letter to more than 3,000 people announcing that after many years of effort and prayer, we had chosen to separate. A chill went down several hundred spines that day, as people opened their mail to learn about the brokenness that existed in their pastors' lives. Such an announcement would have been quite a bombshell under any circumstances, since we are both Christian pastors who believe in the institution of marriage and since most folks knew little or nothing of our married life and therefore did not see it coming. However, further complicating matters in this instance was the fact that June and I were each appointed as pastors of this same congregation. The letter was not simply from a pastor. It was from two of their pastors.

There was a time very recently when, in most North American churches, such an announcement would have been accompanied or followed by an immediate change of pastoral assignments at the very least. Very often, such a turn in a pastor's life meant it was time to get a real estate license, to find another trade. Grassroots sentiment is shifting almost everywhere as significant numbers of folks have either divorced themselves or experienced the pain of divorce in the lives of friends and family. Each church and denomination has to prayerfully consider the best way to approach the issue of pastoral divorce, both in terms of general policy and in terms of the individual cases, no two of which are the same.

In our case, June and I each expressed our willingness to move on to new ministry challenges if our congregation's leadership team felt that this was in the church's best interest. However, our church's leadership team unanimously asked our bishop to reappoint both of us as pastors at Gulf Breeze. They weighed all the factors they could weigh, ranging from what they knew about each of us to what our faith teaches us, and they made a tough call. Other equally fine leadership teams at other churches would have made a different call.

My point is simply that the journey since the day when we announced our separation has been truly remarkable for both June and me. For more than two years, we have continued to serve the same congregation as peers and pastoral colleagues. But what has been even more amazing is the way people rallied around us with love and support, even those who were deeply disturbed by the idea of their pastors divorcing. In this incredibly difficult and awkward adjustment, our family was surrounded by prayers for our healing. What could have conceivably been a significant blow to our church's ministry was used by God as a time for healing.

Why would a church choose to keep each side of a divorcing couple as a part of their pastoral team? Certainly, the seven years of pastoral relationships prior to our separation were a factor in the church's decision. Each of us enjoyed positive and effective ministries at Gulf Breeze. But more important still was the fact that our church had come to understand that it was a place of healing, a place where people find wholeness for themselves in our collective brokenness. Years of emphasis on healing had created an environment where people were more prone to love their pastors than to judge them.

On the Sunday after the aforementioned letters went in the mail, by chance I found myself preaching from 1 Peter 2:24 where it reads, "by his wounds you have been healed." I made reference to Henri Nouwen's idea in *The Wounded Healer* that sometimes God's healing doesn't entirely remove the scars of our afflictions, be they emotional or physical. But God makes us more ready and able to bind up the wounds of others because of our experience. I realized as I said these words that I was, at this very same moment, receiving the love of a people who were ready and able to bind up my wounds because so many of them had entered our church community as wounded people themselves and had been touched by God's mercy. I looked all around that room, and to use John Wimber's terms, they were *"doing the stuff."* They were loving me and cheering for me, the way I have loved and cheered for them.

What a time of discovery for all of us! Perhaps the most significant discovery for me personally was that most people, especially the new-to-church people, really didn't care as much about the end of my marriage so much as they cared about my keeping the faith and doing the best I could to be a father and a pastor, a friend and a human being. Through this experience, I became more human and more approachable for many people. June's experience has been similar.

As healing has become an increasingly intentional part of our church's mission, there has been an explosion of specific healing ministries. One of the earliest ministries was the opening of our church's doors to recovery groups such as Alcoholics Anonymous and Alanon. Due to our partnership with such groups, our church has accumulated a significant population of persons "in recovery" of one sort or another. These people, as a group, are more grace-oriented than the average Christian, and offer an important component of our church's personality.

I debated for some time whether or not this book was an appropriate place to share such personal information. I concluded that I could not talk about the ministry of healing or my church's commitment to it without sharing how this commitment has impacted my own life. June concurred with me on this point and encouraged me to share our story. I am now more than a healer. As a part of a healing community, I have been one of those to experience healing. To talk about everyone else's healing and to neglect my own would feel dishonest.

Putting It All Together

These three dynamic ministry themes, hospitality, hope, and healing all came together for our church in 1992. Herb

Sadler was attending a meeting of the United Methodist General Board of Discipleship, when he was asked to define his understanding of evangelism. He thought briefly, reflecting on his experience as pastor at Gulf Breeze. Evangelism, he said, was really a combination of three things: offering God's hospitality, hope, and healing to people who need these things. When Herb got home from that meeting, he presented the three themes to the church in a Sunday message.

In January of 1995, I led a process whereby these themes were placed at the heart of our church's mission statement. At a church leadership conference we hosted in 1998, one of the participants decided to test how deeply this sense of mission was rooted in our people. During breaks, he walked up to random volunteers, at the book table or in the refreshment area and he would ask them point blank: "What would you say is the mission of this church?" They each replied referencing those three words: hospitality, hope, and healing.

Like most pastors, I have often asked the question, "Why do some churches grow and others decline?" I have never been able to peg the answer entirely on theology, because I have seen different kinds of churches grow. I have never been satisfied to peg the answer entirely on sociology and demographics, because I believe that all churches are called to reach out and grow, serving whatever populations God sends to them.

Gulf Breeze is not Plano, Texas, or Marietta, Georgia. It is not Naperville, Illinois, or Moreno Valley, California. These areas have seen enormous population growth in the last decade, and have proven to be fertile soil for church growth and development. By contrast, most churches in our community are not growing. The population in our area has peaked in all but the far eastern end of our community.

And yet, a church affiliated with a mainline denomination, located in an area of limited population, is thriving despite national trends. Not only thriving, but steadily growing, celebrating, giving, sharing, and cutting across ideological, social, and political lines. This church has thrived because it has sought to embody hospitality, hope, and healing for all who come in contact with it. The embodiment of this mission is the major difference between it and most of the neighboring churches which are plateaued or dying.

CHAPTER FOUR

Until the Pastor Is Ready, the Church Isn't Ready

We Were Only Prepared for Yesterday

When I left my home town after college at the age of twenty to go to seminary, an older pastor said to me, "Paul, take lots of Bible in seminary. You can always figure out how to run a mimeograph machine on the job." At the time, I thought this was an odd piece of advice. Now, fifteen years out of seminary, I look back with deep appreciation for the biblical and theological foundations I learned there. And even though I attended one of the more progressive seminaries in North America at the time, I am now aware that most of what I was taught in terms of practical ministry skills are now as outdated as mimeograph machines. I graduated from seminary in 1986, ready for ministry in *1976*. The how-to's are changing in pastoral ministry, faster in my lifetime than perhaps ever before.

I soon discovered that in my denominational tradition, it was the bishop, and not the seminary, who provided me with a job. And so I learned what the bishop wanted in a pastor. He really didn't care if I could preach. In the first fifteen years beyond seminary, no bishop ever heard me preach. The bishop just wanted (1) for my church's membership to increase in number, (2) for my church to pay one hundred percent of its denominational dues, and (3) for me to get along with folks well enough that his phone did not ring with complaints. This was a different set of skills than they taught me in school, but I learned well.

In my first solo pastorate, the town's population collapsed and along with it, the church's finances. Yet, we paid the denominational dues in full, even to the detriment of the local church. I learned to manage the membership numbers so that they always went up at year-end whether we were growing or not. I'll never forget handing in my annual report at the end of one particularly grim year. My church was in a nose-dive, yet official membership was up by seven and our denominational dues had been three-fourths paid, at considerable sacrifice on the part of my church. The district superintendent, my pastoral supervisor, received the report in hand and then looked at me with a smile and said in a chipper tone, "Great year, Paul." I was as much "a company man" in my denomination as my grandfather had been for forty years with Mobil Oil. I was ready now for ministry in the bureaucratic culture of *1966*.

It took me several years beyond seminary to figure out how to be what the churches I served really wanted in a pastor—they wanted a chaplain. I learned that if you could preach effectively, they would tolerate a relatively poor chaplain. Everybody agreed that I could preach. But in both of my first two churches, I followed pastors who had lived their lives drinking coffee in members' kitchens, almost like extended family members. The problem was that I wasn't wired or called to spend my life making small talk in people's kitchens. (I later found that this wasn't necessarily a problem.)

A pastor down the road from that first solo pastorate was thirty years my senior and cared enough to mentor me in how to keep a small-town church happy. He was very kind to me during the hardest years of my life, when I wondered aloud if I was even in the right profession. He taught me how to sit and visit with little old ladies at 2:00 in the afternoon, sipping coffee and pretending to be awake. (The key is in the way you hold your coffee cup, not holding the handle; but, rather, the cup itself, almost to the point of burning your fingers. It is impossible to doze off with burning fingers, even when the heat in the house is turned up to eighty-five degrees.) They had taught me none of this in seminary of course. I learned it all grudgingly, and within a few years, I graduated from small-town duty, ready for ministry not in 1976, but in *1956*. The trouble was that we were now racing toward 1996.

Thus, by my thirtieth birthday, I probably knew even less about effective ministry than I had known when I was fifteen. Both the academy and the church were training me for ministry in the world of yesterday. I had been trained to be a good Christendom pastor, in a post-Christendom world. I had been trained for failure in the twenty-first century. Certainly, there was a time when mentoring by traditional seminaries, denominations, and rural churches worked in producing effective pastors. But that was before my time.

Looking at Life through Mainline Glasses

As I became indoctrinated by the ways of the mainline church in America, I became somewhat distrustful of growing churches; fascinated by them, but leery of them, almost sure that they must be cheating somewhere. By cheating, I mean breaking the rules: offering cheap, easy-answer theology or entertainment-oriented worship, shortcutting denominational emphases and connections, and/or preaching with no lectionary.

Through three diverse pastoral assignments and my doctoral studies, I failed to find any significant data that would offer hope to either the future of the mainline churches or their ability to effectively connect with the unchurched. Like two highways veering off from a junction, the church I knew was going one way and the dominant cultures another, never again to cross paths. The only exceptions that I saw to the general pattern of decline in Christian communities fell into three categories: they were marked by (1) a hyperactive, over-functioning pastor, (2) right-wing theology and politics, and/or (3) a neighborhood setting where new houses were going in by the hundreds all around the church.

Please do not misunderstand me. It is not as if the churches I served during the early years of my ministry were dead. On the contrary, good things happened in each place. In each place I found people who loved the Lord. In each place, I saw a few lives transformed. We were just so shackled by tradition and insider culture that it was like trying to run a sack race. We bumbled along. We needed to take a deep drink from Hebrews 12, where we are encouraged to throw off everything that hinders us in our race. But even then, I am not sure that we would have known immediately what to hold on to and what to throw off. We probably would have just held on to everything, just in case.

Obviously, when we hold on to everything, cultural gaps between the congregation and the larger village usually widen. We often grow older and more affluent than most of the people in our communities. In many cases, our preferred music, our way of dress, and our automobiles in the church parking lot communicate to all that we are a culture of old people with money. In other cases, simply that we are old. In certain settings, this transformation from community church to holy fortress has been a gradual process, spanning several generations. In other places, it has happened in less than two decades. Even community outreach has become distanced from the inner fellowship and worship life of many congregations.

There was, in each of the churches that I served, an honest desire to meet the spiritual needs of the wider community. But the only way we knew to attempt this was on our own cultural terms. We expected people to come onto our turf, at a time convenient for us, to sing our music, to sit on our benches, and watch us parade around in robes.

As a thirty-year-old pastor of a small-town First Church, I looked forward to growing in ministry through job promotion from church to church. I hoped that one of the churches along the way might grow, but I was unable to imagine a church thriving and growing to the point that I could stay and grow with it. My father had been pastor of a similar small-town church a quarter of a century earlier. One day, when he was exceedingly frustrated by the small thinking and the lack of vision, his youth minister said to him, "Just think, Preacher, in a few more years, you can get a big one of these."

Here is a classified ad, which appeared in *Christian Century* magazine a couple years ago, looking for a pastor for a "bigger one of these." It speaks volumes about what mainline churches and pastors tend to value.

> **SENIOR PASTOR/HEAD OF STAFF** An urban church on a handsome, historic residential avenue, X Church is known for its scholarly and strong preaching, traditional worship style, fine music, and membership composed of civic and academic leaders. Well functioning and financially healthy, X Church has a self-directed, competent staff in place, a strong church school, focused and ever-growing outreach, and myriad opportunities for fellowship, education and service for all ages. We desire leadership that guides us with the spiritual power of dynamic preaching and the secular competence of a wise, effective leader and manager. (Christian Century, Jan 27, 1999, p. 87)

What does this ad teach us?

1. This church values its status as a private, elite institution in terms of its address, its intellectualism, its history, its upper crust formality, its organization, its money, and its connection to high society. They not only have a cultural gap between themselves and the community, they are proud of the gap! Whatever the outreach they refer to, this is decidedly not an open-door church.
2. The staff is entrenched, competent or not.

3. This church does not desire to be led anywhere. Leadership is about change; yet this church is very content with the way things are.

This is typical of the high steeple churches that too often serve as models to scores of other churches in their denominational families or region. If this ad had appeared several years earlier, I might have thrown my name in the hat.

God Had Other Plans

In the winter of 1993, I was racing through my office one afternoon about to leave for a denominational committee meeting with the bishop, when I noticed that the answering machine was blinking. Among the messages, I found one from a fellow named Herb Sadler in a place called Gulf Breeze, Florida. Though he didn't say what he wanted, and though no one had ever tried to recruit me from beyond my region, I immediately had a hunch what he was calling about. I stopped, returned his call and the hunch was confirmed.

Three weeks later, I was in Florida, interviewing with a new congregation about going there to serve as associate pastor. I prayed about it. They prayed about it. We all believed God was in it and we cut a deal. We spent the next several months trying to get two bishops (one in Dallas and one in Montgomery, Alabama) to allow the deal to transpire. The Texas bishop told me that it was a mistake for me to go, that I would be starting all over again, that I would end up taking a pay cut and then get sent to an even smaller town than the one I was serving at the time. The Alabama bishop dragged his feet for two months in making the appointment. The church I was leaving had been assigned to another pastor, but still no word from the bishop as to whether we would be allowed to make the move. In fact, we signed a contract on a house, still without any official word from the bishop. In cutting a deal directly with me, Gulf Breeze Church was acknowledging that they knew more about what they needed in a pastor than a denominational executive.

My peers in ministry were not much more encouraging than the bishops. It's interesting, the things that pastors say to one another. We ought to listen to ourselves on tape occasionally in such conversations. This is what I heard: "You are a leader; you don't need to be number two." "You are rising up the ladder. You have established your name in this region. To go across the nation will be like starting over." "Associate pastors are apprentices. You are past that." "Just be sure, at least, that you are number two and that they put it in writing." Those last words of wisdom were from my father. Each of these statements belied an assumption that pastoral ministry is by nature a solo effort. The concept of a pastoral team, in which there were multiple pulpit voices and multiple leaders, was a new concept to a lot of folks in 1993. In the next few years, however, Gulf Breeze would join with Willow Creek Church and a host of churches across North America, in becoming team-led.

The move from working in isolation to working as a team was very refreshing for me. My ministry colleagues were no longer primarily the pastors down the road, but the staff members playing on my team. The competitiveness that I had known among ministry peers all the way back to seminary days was gone. Furthermore, I discovered a church culture where members were not resisting innovation. So my relationship with key lay leadership became far more trusting as well. This isn't to say that there weren't still occasional angry, unhappy personalities lashing out at the church or the pastors. But in a team setting, my family and I were far more buffered from these people than we ever had been in a solo pastor setting. All this is to say that, for me, ministry on a team beats the solo experience hands down.

Nonetheless, I still suffered a bit of culture shock as I came to a very different kind of church. I was, for example, somewhat unaccustomed to other young adults at church, especially male peers at church. In most mainline churches, there are not many men under the age of 40. It took a bit of adjustment to get used to a place where young adult couples were truly engaged in the church's life. It took getting used to a senior pastor who preached from whatever biblical text he wanted to preach from each week rather than from the official lectionary of texts. I kept trying to figure out if Herb Sadler was liberal or conservative. In nine years of working with him, I never have figured that out. He likes it that way. Whenever he is asked to label himself theologically, he has a stock response. "Whatever Jesus is, that's what I want to be." Not a bad answer.

In 1993, Gulf Breeze Church was still relatively traditional in all three of its Sunday worship services, with all music led by an organ, most of it out of the hymnal. Pastors and choirs were robed. There was a predictable order to worship. Had it not been this way, I am certain that I would not have had the nerve to go there at that point in my own development. Worship was traditional, and yet there was tremendous life and playfulness in both the music and the preaching. They were starting to color outside the lines a bit. They had greatly simplified the liturgy. They were ignoring most of the holy days on the denominational calendar except for Easter and Christmas. The concern was not about propagating church culture, but rather, about bringing hope to the people present.

I discovered a church where ministry was driven neither by some seminary's agenda nor by a denomination's agenda. And, because this church had retained the same senior pastor for eighteen years at that point, he had been able to lead them beyond the agenda of the congregation's controlling personalities. Within a few months, the challenge of ministry began to look very different to me. It was as if scales came off my eyes.

The Issue of Our Deepest Loyalty

One of the major issues that had been hindering me as I "ran my race" prior to this point was my desire to prove my loyalty to the denominational system that employed me. I wanted to talk a certain way and to embrace the right tradition. I wanted to look United Methodist. I wanted to be loyal. I realize now that this was a choice to be less effective in many instances. Had I served my previous pastoral appointments with a different understanding of where the critical points of loyalty lied, I believe I could have been more effective in building those churches and in reaching the communities which surrounded those churches.

Here is how I understand denominational loyalty these days, within my own denominational context.

1. *Loyalty means that a denominationally-affiliated congregation offers its full and fair share of support to the denomination's shared ministry most of the time.* In our denomination, we are billed for this. In other settings, congregations set this amount freely. In most United Methodist congregations, dues to our denomination (called "apportionments") add up to around seventeen percent of general offering proceeds. We pay these causes quietly and faithfully, and in so doing we network with other churches in our denomination on a myriad of great causes; we also feed and water the denominational bureaucracies. Gulf Breeze Church, however, is aware that it would not be where it is today, had not the local leadership *once* chosen to pay considerably less than was asked of it, in order that the present sanctuary could be built. They made a hard call and a right call that year, and did so over a bishop's protest. There was not enough money to pay the denomination and to build the building they so desperately needed for their future. That building became a critical conduit to so much of the future growth. The church in 1983 simply said that it believed the most important thing was embracing its future as a regional church. The denomination went unpaid in some areas for a

couple years. As a result of that choice, we became able to pay far more than any other church in our district to support denominational causes. This congregation grew to be a major pipeline of financial support for the ministries of our denomination.

2. *Loyalty to denomination means that a congregation embraces the doctrinal emphases and flavor that come from its unique and special stream of Christian heritage.* In our case, this heritage is the Wesleyan stream of church tradition. Each congregation will interface with this doctrinal heritage differently. Nevertheless, loyalty to the people who brought us to this point means we can frame our beliefs with a solid awareness of and even reference to our particular heritages. We can also be pragmatic. We do not do things a set way simply because we have always done them that way, or say things a set way, because we have always said them that way. Often we find new ways to do and to say key things. When this happens, it is usually rooted in the answer to the question "Why?" We ask, "Why is it we have done this thing this way all these years?" If the answer is related to bedrock of Christian belief, we don't change. But insofar as the answer is related to cultural or historical considerations, we are open to review and to alter the way we do something, so that it expresses the Christian good news more clearly in our cultural context. We can feel free to clap for a newly baptized baby rather than read in unison some canned thing out of the hymnal. We can feel free to greatly simplify the invitation to Holy Communion, changing it each time we gather together, yet still retaining the integrity and essence of the liturgy.

You would most likely never find a course offered at Gulf Breeze Church entitled, "What It Means to Be a United Methodist." We are not in the business of making Methodists. We make Christians, plain and simple. We make disciples of Jesus.

3. *Loyalty to denomination means offering quality worship experiences which are as effective today in lifting up Christ and*

drawing people to him as were the worship experiences back in the early days when a denomination movement was born. Many, if not most, denominational movements were born out of moments when worship was alive and life-changing for the participants. Loyalty to a denominational tradition is less related to singing the same songs Luther sang than it is to applying many of the same principles to worship today that Luther and company applied to Reformation worship in the late 1500s. There is no compelling reason why there should be uniformity of liturgy from church to church within a denomination. Many churches can write their own formats for baptism, confirmation, and communion. As I have helped to write fresh liturgies for such events, it has always been with reference to the traditional United Methodist liturgies. Certain wording can be retained as a conscious tie-in to our liturgical heritage. However, I am convinced that using ineffective and obsolete wording in worship has nothing to do with being a loyal United Methodist, a loyal Presbyterian, or a loyal anything else.

4. Loyalty to denomination means sending a congregation's people to participate in those gatherings and committees that we believe are truly helpful to our congregation's mission. Attending every denominational gathering offered has nothing to do with being loyal to one's denomination. Not every meeting is helpful for every congregation or for every pastor. Occasionally, there are gatherings that are not helpful to me or to my church, but which offer an opportunity where I can be helpful to the larger body. Those gatherings are rare. Most of the time, if a meeting is not helpful to what I am about in ministry, I need to avoid that meeting. I can still be thankful for the ways that the denomination strives to provide resources for local churches, especially smaller congregations. A very large congregation has needs and ways of doing ministry which are often very different from the vast majority of congregations in a denominational family. Large and/or highly self-defined congregations need to link up with other like churches. Or if this is not feasible, such congregations may choose to do their own thing when it comes to camps, retreats, leadership training, mission projects, etc.

5. *Loyalty to denomination means praying for our denomination.* I still remember a promise I made somewhere back there to pray for my church, and I do so, at both the congregational and the denominational level. I pray for my bishop and for missionaries and for leadership at all levels of church life. I pray for leaders and ministries in my own local congregation. Diligent praying is probably the greatest single thing I can do to express love and loyalty to my church and denomination.

6. *In the United Methodist setting, loyalty to denomination means I am committed to serve as pastor wherever the bishop sends me.* I am appointed by my bishop each year to a pastoral assignment. If the bishop were to desire to move one of us from the pastoral team at Gulf Breeze, it would need to be in close consultation with the team itself. If any of us had grave misgivings about the proposed appointment, we would certainly say so. Herb Sadler has resisted attempts by bishops to move him on at least three occasions. Pastoral changes can be very destabilizing to congregations. Bishops who do not listen carefully to pastors and lay leadership in the appointive process can gravely wound the ministries of extraordinary churches. Yet, United Methodist bishops are empowered to make the final call about the assignments of pastors. Until such a day as our General Conference changes that reality, we who are pastors in my denomination had best make peace within our souls and within our families about this. And if there is no peace, we pastors always have the option of serving in a setting outside the United Methodist umbrella.

7. *A pastor's denominational loyalty is best reflected in the building of strong congregations within the denominational family.* My highest earthly loyalty as a pastor is not to a bishop, but to the soul of the community where I have been appointed to serve as pastor. This is new for me. Before I

came to Gulf Breeze, I had been taught that the most basic building block of United Methodist life was the annual conference. Too much of my energy and concern was directed to concerns beyond the most important thing, beyond the task of building a church in the place I was planted. The basic building block of any denomination is the local church. My first commitment now is to the health of local churches, specifically to helping build the congregation where I am appointed as a pastor, so that it can effectively reach new people with the good news. Insofar as denominational connections contribute directly to the effectiveness at the local church level, I am eager to support those connections.

Herb and I each destroyed our moving boxes the week after we moved in. No need to save them. We came to stay a long time. I used to read the annual conference journal (where local church statistical tables appear and pastoral salaries are listed) and speculate about my next appointment. In recent times, I have gone for years without opening such a journal. If I need such information, I know where to find it. But I have established the habit of living my days with the basic assumption that my next appointment is my present appointment. In Lyle Schaller's insightful book, *The Very Large Church,* he tells the story of a pastor who had served five different churches over his career, only to reveal at the end of the story that it had been the same church, growing to different stages, demanding different skills of the pastor at each turn. In pastoral ministry, certainly there is a time for moving and a time for staying. But we ought to approach ministry always assuming it's a time for staying, unless day-to-day experience begins to teach us otherwise. Then it's time to take up the matter with God and with trusted counsel. Often, after praying through an issue, God will send us back to minister in a tough situation. Other times, God grants a sense of release, making it appropriate to pursue a change in pastoral assignments.

If I were a leader in a local church who honestly felt that the bishop, in an appointment of a pastor to my church, was harming my church, I would protest with every ounce of energy within me. I see nothing disloyal in loving one's church and wanting it to have a good future. I see nothing disloyal in feeling a vested interest in the selection of a new pastor. United Methodist church law may give the full power of pastoral selection to a bishop, but our tradition also embraces the freedom of people to speak their conscience. There is nothing disloyal about that.

As of this writing, there are three large congregations in this region of my denomination who have retained senior pastors for more than twenty years each. We are fortunate that our bishops have recognized the reality that to have moved these pastors would have severely impacted the future growth of these congregations. The combined average attendance of these three churches at the time their present senior pastors were first appointed to each was about 350 total people between the three churches. (These churches are: Christ United Methodist Church in Mobile, Alabama; Frazer Memorial United Methodist Church in Montgomery, Alabama; and Gulf Breeze Church. There were about 250 a week at Frazer, less than 100 at Gulf Breeze, and none at Christ Church because its present pastor founded it.) Last year, the combined average attendance of these three churches was in excess of 8,000.

A pastor needs to put down roots in a place, to really fall in love with a place, and to fall in love with the people in that place. If a pastor can't do that, he/she is either in the wrong place, or the wrong line of work.

If you are a pastor, ask yourself this all-important question: Where do your real loyalties lie? And how are these loyalties expressed in your leadership and behavior? If your real loyalty is to a theological system, to a denominational machine, or to an ideological perspective, people will see this easily enough. If, on the other hand, your real loyalty is to help people experience the hospitality, hope, and healing of Jesus Christ, they will see that.

Holy Vision and Lots of Love

There are, these days, a myriad of pastors learning the same lessons that I have learned, discovering mid-stream that the rules of effective ministry are changing. I see them everywhere, trying to turn around established churches. As a part of the team at Easum, Bandy and Associates, I hear pastors from across North America sharing the pain and loneliness of turning around stagnant and declining congregations. As a group, the pastors who plant churches are faring much better in the fruits of their labors than those pastors who are seeking to turn around established churches.

I have never been a true turn around pastor, who has led a long stagnated church into a period of extended vitality and growth. I have immense respect for turn around pastors. The ship that I have helped to steer for the last nine years was turned around long before I came on board. But I work with the pastor who turned it around. I also have shared in some major changes of course, which are continually necessary, even in very vital churches, in order to ensure a vital and productive future. Based on these experiences, I have concluded that there are two critical ingredients in the effective leadership of established congregations (an established congregation being a church that (1) is more than ten years old, (2) has constructed a building and been in it for at least a year, or (3) is no longer being led by the founding pastor).

These ingredients are holy vision and love. Holy vision is something that God gives. It doesn't come necessarily from the latest fad or the highest profile teaching church. It can't be found in books or continuing education events. It does require time, Bible, and prayer. Many pastors are too busy with endless details to tend to their vision. Most pastors are too tired to vision. Visioning is both a lone enterprise and a team enterprise. But it is clear that none of us do it well on the run. Pastors and leadership teams need to set aside regular time away from the hurricane of ministry. In this time, they can rest, they can listen, they can laugh, and they can gain perspective.

Biblically, the patterns are clear and famous. From Moses to Jesus, God formed the greatest leaders in the desert, away from the busyness of life. Jesus, in particular, had a habit of regular, daily retreat, in which his spirit and his clarity of purpose were renewed. If Jesus needed such time, how on earth do we reason that we can lead effectively without it?

I meet a lot of pastors who are floundering and clueless as to what to do next. In almost every case, that pastor is exhausted. I find it no accident that almost every significant idea or answer to a dilemma that I have faced in ministry has come to me either while I was out of town or in a retreat setting.

But the power of holy vision does not center simply on the moment that vision dawns. Once we discover anew what God is calling us to be and do, we have to keep an eye on that calling, and allow it to form our schedules, our priorities, and our behaviors.

I meet just as many pastors who have a clear vision as I do pastors who are floundering. But most of these visionary pastors, in established churches, are frustrated. In most situations, there are controlling powers, both locally in the church, and often within the denominational hierarchy, who do not share the vision and may seek to block it at every turn. So the truth is that holy vision alone does not an effective pastor make. Something more is needed.

I believe that *missing something* is love. Too often, the leader(s) go up on the mountain and get the vision and then come down to butt heads with the people. In such a confrontation, one of two things happens: the leader(s) either run off the people who oppose the vision or the opposition neutralizes the leader, possibly even running him/her off. If you are a pastor, new to an established church, ready to spend your bullets on a vision that the old guard leaders in that church do not buy into, odds are that in five years, the people who oppose you will still be there and you will be gone. Most likely, you will leave out of frustration. Maybe you will get fired. In either case, you will have failed to lead that church anywhere.

Rabbi Edwin Friedman in his landmark work on pastoral leadership, *Generation to Generation*, reminded us that we can lead most effectively when we couple a strong sense of where to go with love. Effective turn around pastors need to take time to build relationships with two kinds of leaders in the church. First, they need to invest some time with the leaders who gravitate toward the vision, many of whom may be new leaders. My dad used to say, "Move with the movers." It was his way of saying, find the people who are ready to move in the direction you are leading and grow them, all the while allowing them to feed you as well. But there is another group of leaders who are just as important—these are the people who may or may not have the vision, but they have the resources to make some things happen or to keep things from happening. Some of them are controlling and negative by nature. Others of them are just "old-timers" who carry clout with a host of people. Still others are leaders in the community, who have the potential to open doors that are not easily opened without them. Still others are sitting on financial resources that if unleashed for God, could help to fuel major ministry expansion.

Two groups: the people who get it, and the people who don't get it yet, but who, when they do, could turn the world upside down. Pastors need to invest in relationships with the second group. Pastors need to love these people. Go to lunch with these people. Play with these people. Pray for these people, by name. Invest some time early on with the people who hold the keys to the future of the congregation. Rarely will we win all of them. But often, even the most controlling of leaders invested in the status quo of a church can come around in time *if we love them.*

Furthermore, beyond investment in leaders, the first few months of a pastor's tenure should enable multiple opportunities for pastors to meet as many of the congregation as possible in social settings. Ken Callahan in his book, *New Beginnings for Pastors and Congregations,* sets forth a great plan for how to build strong pastoral relationships in the early days of a new pastoral assignment. When people experience their pastor as a fun human being who cares about them, who cares to learn their names and to learn about their work and their lives, then they perceive that pastor differently. Say a pastor's preaching quality is a five on the one-to-ten scale. If that pastor has weak relationships with the congregation, the five may be perceived as a two or a three. However, the people who have come to know and love that pastor will hear the same sermon and perceive it as a seven or an eight. Early investments in caring relationships with people buy credibility for the pastor, credibility that will be needed for constructive change in the months and years ahead.

Over the years, less and less of an effective pastor's time will be focused on caring for "all the sheep in the flock," and more and more time will be focused on the nurturing of leaders. However, the wise pastor knows that in the first week of a new pastorate, spending some quality time at the local hospital is much more helpful than unpacking books, in terms of building credibility for pastoral leadership in a community. Books can always be unpacked later. First impressions about caring are not easily unlearned.

I am not advocating a return to the chaplaincy model of ministry. The chaplaincy model that is failing the church on all fronts today is the model where the pastor tries to do all the caring in the church. This results in aimless, under-functioning churches, where members do not adequately develop their gifts and skills to do ministry. The chaplaincy model creates an unhealthy dependency on the pastor.

But pastors still need to care about people. We may gradually give away the hospital ministry, but we still need to go to the hospital occasionally. We need to love our leaders in order to be leaders of leaders. Some people will complain that the pastor has picked favorites. Let them complain. None of us can be friends with everyone. Jesus certainly picked people with whom he invested his time.

If people know I love them, they are more apt to tolerate my leadership when it moves against their preferred patterns and instincts. If people know I love them, they are more apt to want to behave in ways that will nurture and encourage my continued love. When I love people as their pastor, they give me some slack to innovate. The longer these relationships last, the greater the chance that I will be there when the youngest daughter marries or when the family patriarch has brain surgery. The longer these relationships last, the greater the chance that we will have taken a trip together or experienced a significant event together, after which mutual fond memories remain. People don't forget these things.

Bishops and search committees assign pastors to congregations. But they don't make pastors. They nominate men and women to be pastors. Pastors, however, are made after they arrive in a town. It is like running for president. We won't be elected, perhaps, for several months, until the consensus develops among the people that we are God's appointed pastoral leader for the days and years ahead. This mantle of leadership is conferred on us only after we have been in place for a while; after we have established effective and satisfying relationships.

The main reason that Gulf Breeze Church was able, at the ripe old age of forty-two, to choose a multi-campus ministry is because of years of careful, pastoral loving of the key leaders and stake holders in our church. When the idea about the East Campus came down, some people got really upset. The project could have prevailed without those people. As pastors we could have said, "Let them go. We can live without them." We could indeed have lived without them. None of us, not even pastors, are indispensable to God's work.

In most turn around churches, there will be persons who must leave a church as a part of the turn around and revitalization. It is certainly better for the church to move forward without them and do the right thing than to wait for one hundred percent consensus. Waiting for unanimity allows those who do not fully embrace the vision to veto the church's future. Early on in the Gulf Breeze turn around, there were several families who left because they disagreed with key decisions the church made at the time. I felt certain we would lose a few members over the East Campus issue. In the end, however, no one left the church over our decision to go multi-campus. And this is why: our leadership, pastors included, sat down with the detractors and the people who were pained over the church's direction and we let them talk. We listened and listened in various settings. We clarified misinformation. We agreed to disagree on certain things. But we listened, and we allowed those people to know that we heard their concerns. They were old-timers, many of them. They loved their church and their pastors. And they knew that their pastors loved them. In the end, most of their worst-case worries proved unfounded and they relaxed. Most of them grew to embrace the vision of the Community Life Center, and a few became very vocal advocates on behalf of the new ministries that were based there. Gulf Breeze Church is richer today because those folks stayed around. They are good people, giving people, deeply spiritual people, who are engaged in a lot of great ministry in our community. They simply didn't understand what we were doing for a moment, but we loved them through it.

Some pastors will read this and say, "I can't bear the thought of caring for these obstinate people." But please, take note, this is not an issue of temperament or spiritual gifts. Mercy is a spiritual gift listed by the apostle Paul. By every measure, I do not have this gift. Empathy sometimes runs a bit shallow in me. But still I am *commanded* to love. Love is not a spiritual gift. It is the great commandment. It is more about doing than about feeling. The commandment to love comes straight from Jesus, who told us it was the most important thing of all. Pastors, we are supposed to love our churches. Loving our people is not chaplaincy. It is not passive acquiescence to the status quo. Love means praying for our leaders, and perhaps, in tough times, telling them that we are doing so. Love means acting out of principle, not out of emotional knee-jerk reaction. Love means looking for the good in the hearts of those who oppose us. Love means treating those people with kindness and respect, even as we seek to lead in ways they oppose. People can tell, most of the time, when they are loved and when they are not. And when they are loved, they are far more likely to accept a pastor's leadership.

In thinking back to that small-town church I mentioned at the beginning of this chapter, the one that wanted a chaplain—what they really needed was to be loved. And these are not the same things. I finally succeeded in being the chaplain—being present at the hospital, the funeral home, drinking coffee in the kitchens—but I am not sure that I ever loved those people as I should have. That is one of the most sincere regrets that I have in my life. It is little wonder that we failed to accomplish much together.

Just as holy vision is something that only God can give, the same should be said about love. Love is something from beyond me, that comes to me, that passes through me. It's a God thing, plain and simple. But I have to be open to it and disciplined about it.

Our love does not stop with congregational members and leaders. I am not sure it is even supposed to start there. If we use God's love as a model for how we ought to love, we should consider these words from John 3:16, which are the foundation of our faith: "For God so loved the world . . ." As I look at effective pastors in all sorts of settings, I see pastors who love their communities. I said it a few pages back. I will say it again. Pastors need to fall in love with their communities.

One of the reasons that pastors accomplish so much more in newly planted churches than in established congregations is that most church planters have chosen their little spot of soil over all the other places in the world. They usually have a multi-dimensional love for the place that will help to hold them there for a long time. They have a natural desire to communicate in the local vernacular and to lead ministry to touch the most apparent local needs.

Jim Griffith, one of founders of Willow Creek Church and one of the leading coaches to church planters in America, shared this observation with me: "People know quickly whether the planter likes the area or just sees them as an objective to be accomplished. I call this affinity for the area. Do they like the people, i.e., their culture, their values, their hobbies, their festivals, their sports teams, etc.? Those planters (and/or spouses) that don't really like the area they are trying to reach will certainly fail."

This principle is just as true in effective pastorates of established churches as it is in church plants. Too often pastors go to a place simply because an external authority has sent them there or because they are looking for a job. It is wise to ask, "Does this pastoral candidate and family really want to be here more than anyplace else in the world?"

Am I Ready to Lead?

Until pastors are ready to lead, their churches cannot be ready to go anywhere. We can point in many directions looking for clues as to why some churches thrive and other churches wither. When we neutralize differences in demographics and theology, some churches still outperform expectations and others underperform. There are only two remaining reasons to explain the difference between churches: leadership and the Holy Spirit. We don't have any control over the Holy Spirit. Neither do we create the demographics or the theological traditions in which we work. The one thing I can have control over is myself. I can get ready to lead and stay ready. An awful lot of us in church leadership are not ready for twenty-first century ministry.

To get ready, I would suggest we do the following things.

1. Have a little funeral for Christendom. Take some symbols of the way Christendom has taught you to be a pastor and go bury those things in the backyard. Dig a little hole. You may want to invite friends and family. Or you may want to have a private service, just you and God. Consider what objects you can bury, which will symbolize an era of ministry that has passed away forever. Possibilities include your tradition's book of worship, or any number of books on your library shelves dealing with ministry the way we were taught in seminary. If your church is stuck in the archaic practice of pinning ribbons on the lapels of visitors, get a handful of those and throw them in the hole as well. If your church has a strategic plan that spans more than two years, tear off everything dealing with years three and beyond, and throw that in the hole. If your denominational judicatory has an annual journal, you may still need a phone number or two, but throw last year's edition in the hole to remind yourself that all those statistics and committee reports mean nothing to God. Take your congregation's list of church officers and committee members and throw it in as well. Mark the fact that God doesn't do business by committee anymore. If he ever did. Throw in a coffee cup for good measure to symbolize the death of chaplaincy as a viable leadership strategy. Be creative. Be bold. And you may be surprised at the power you feel as you shovel the dirt on top of these symbols of yesterday. Say a prayer of thanks for God's blessings in the 1,600 years passing away, and go in peace to face your future.

2. Walk the streets of the community you serve. Walk and pray. Ask God to show you what his will is for this place. Ask him what he wants to happen, and dare to throw yourself in the middle of it. Too often we come up with plans and ask God to bless them. We need to turn that around. As you walk, ask God to enable you to fall in love with that place and with the people who live there, or to send you to another place.

3. Each week, stop working at the busyness of pastoring after forty hours. Period. Most effective pastors (not counting bivocationals) work about fifty to fifty-five hours a week. Many work a lot less than that. The last ten to fifteen hours should be spent in prayer or in a fishing boat. This will be a major shift for many of us. But without it, there is little chance that God can change us and form us into leaders. If you are a board member or leader in your local church, sit your pastor down and insist on this point. Send that pastor away after forty hours to pray, to play, to rest, and to grow as a human being. Your church will be so much richer for doing this. Of course, in cooking down our active ministry time to forty hours or less, some tasks will be jettisoned altogether.

4. When God speaks to you, stop and mark the moment! In the fall of 1996, I was sitting in one of worst denominational meetings I've ever had the misfortune of attending, and this talking head was blabbering on about how to reach baby boomers or something. Suddenly I couldn't hear him anymore. I never heard an audible voice from that point on— God's or anyone else's—but I noticed tears starting to run down my face. Mind you, this was odd. I am not particularly emotional, and it was not a holy moment of worship. It was simply God's moment with me. I felt God's love in that moment like I had never felt before. And I heard clearly in my heart, "Paul, I am about to do something in you and through you. Get ready." I had to leave the room. I walked through the hotel lobby and out beyond to the moonlit beach. And I accepted anew the call to ministry that night. I drove home a couple of hours later, and discovered upon walking through the door that my father had died that evening. As I began to piece together the timeline of the evening, his death came at almost exactly the moment that God spoke to me in the hotel ballroom. My dad was a pastor; he was the greatest coach and mentor in ministry that I have had. I had no idea that he was leaving this world at the time God spoke to me. But in retrospect, the meaning of that night was something akin to the experience between Elijah and Elisha. It was a milestone in my life, a moment when my mentor was leaving (even though I did not know it), and God was simultaneously placing a great challenge before me. Five and a half months later, the East Campus project was born. As the project unfolded, I was asked to assume leadership in it.

My point in sharing this story is to underline how God was working in me, calling me, preparing me all along. On days when I am stressed over this or that, or disappointed in some way about something that has happened, I almost always think back to that night when God met me in that crazy hotel meeting. It reminds me of why I am here. It reminds me that none of this is my own doing. It reminds me that God is not blessing my ideas or efforts, but rather that I am participating in God's ideas and efforts. And the timing of it all has given me a joyful sense that my earthly father has been able to share in the joys of what has happened in the years since, as part of the cloud of witnesses above.

5. *Make and keep a list of the people who hold the keys to what God wants to do.* Be intentional in pastoring those people. Love and lead those people. Learn from them as well. They do not have to be church members to make the list. The list I keep always is a mix of members and non-members. You can love most people to just about anywhere you need to lead them.

6. *Read the book of Acts.* If Acts can't stir us, we might as well hang it up. The books of Luke and Acts are really one powerful narrative that show us how the Holy Spirit broke into human life and created the church. Almost every value that I seek to lift up in this book can be found rooted in the book of Acts.

7. *Be positive at all times, even when there just doesn't seem to be anything positive left in you.* The best tool a pastor has for initiating change in the church is a positive spirit that looks

for something to affirm in even the most irritating and back-ward-thinking church member. Be on the lookout for even small signs of hopefulness in the behavior of those you are leading, and celebrate everything you can celebrate! Especially in turn around situations, a commitment to focus on the positive will do wonders to transform the climate of a congregation that has been slowly losing the battle.

8. *Network with other pastors and leaders who are traveling the same direction you are.* You may not find these in your regional denominational gatherings or generic community pastor's fellowships. So cast your eyes on a wider horizon. You may find them at a leadership development event sponsored by groups such as Leadership Network, Net Results, or Easum, Bandy and Associates. You may find them in a focused pastor's fellowship that embraces the values of effective post-Christendom ministry. Increasingly you may find these friends online. The Internet is drawing leaders together from around the world. Wonderful part-nerships and friendships are being born through on-line networks and communities that exist to resource and encourage Christian leaders.

9. *We need to start mentoring others from the beginning.* The main job of leaders is to work themselves out of their job. Transformational pastors are disciplined about making dis-ciples, not generically, but specifically. Such leaders are always asking, "Who can do this?" "Who can take over this ministry or this task?" They are always replacing them-selves. So when either the Lord or the bishop removes them, others are already carrying out most of the critical things they started. The apostle Paul was a master of this. And he left a legacy that has shaken the foundations of many empires. We are ready to begin ministry the day we begin teaching someone else how to do ministry. Don't save mentoring for late in the game. Start multiplying yourself from the beginning.

The Bottom Line

The bottom line in leading is always this: it's difficult to lead to places where we have never been. If we are seeking to lead change in a church, the change needs to happen first in our lives. The old revivalist A. W. Tozer used to talk about spiritual revival like this: we first draw a circle around ourselves and pray for God to bring revival inside the circle. Then we seek to lead and pray for spiritual revival beyond the circle of our own lives.

Until pastors give up obsessing with institution and tradition, it is not likely that they can lead their churches to give up such obsessions. Until pastors become open to the work of God's Spirit, how can they lead their churches to follow the Spirit? Until pastors dare to fling open the doors of their own souls to the precious people God has placed around them, how can they possibly lead their churches to be centers of hospitality to God's stray sheep? Until pastors have been possessed by hope, how can they proclaim hope? Until they have known healing, how can they heal?

It starts with God. And then, God forms leaders. To start at any other point is a recipe for failure.

CHAPTER FIVE

Building a World-Class Leadership Team

The year 1998 was strange for me. The Community Life Center project had been born the year before. Land had been purchased. Architects had begun drawing. Focus groups and surveys had begun to clarify community needs. We were ready to invite our people to make a financial investment. And yet, in many ways, this new ministry initiative was all still a dream. It wasn't real yet. The Community Life Center ministry was, at this point, essentially just me and a bunch of file folders crammed full of ideas, surveys, floor plans, names, and phone numbers. There were no other identified ministry leaders yet. There was no recreation ministry yet, no preschool, no small groups. On the Main Campus, ministry was kicking. But most of the ministries that would be based at the East Campus waited for leaders. It was the closest experience I can imagine to what it must be like to be pregnant.

By late in the year, we had collected about three dozen resumes of job applicants for recreation director and worship/music pastor. But at year-end, we still had not clearly identified one single leader to do anything related to the Community Life Center.

Fast forward two years, and you would find a team of ten core staff members based at the Community Life Center, plus the preschool staff and the myriad of hourly workers and contract workers leading the recreation and child care ministries. In addition, there are so many volunteers, I would not even know how to begin to count them. Together, these leaders, both paid and volunteer, make up one of the most effective ministry teams I have ever witnessed.

In 1999, God pulled this team together. Without this team, we would have simply had a nice building. Without this team, that building, like most new church buildings, would have sat empty most of the time and done very little to advance God's mission in our community.

Effective church leadership teams are powerful combinations of the right paid staff alongside hundreds of others, not on payroll, who live out their gifts and callings in various ministry projects. This chapter deals with strategies for getting and keeping the right staff, as well as creating a climate where staff support and deploy hundreds of others to do ministry.

The Role of Paid Leadership

What is the role of paid staff? Many churches are figuring out that we don't hire staff to do ministry on behalf of everyone else. Rather, *paid staff members exist to coach others in ministry, to lead the leaders.* The larger our church has grown, the fewer ministry ideas seem to originate with individual staff members. Our best new ministries today seem to originate either in the hearts of ordinary people in the church or from the synergy of our leadership team in conversation with each other. It is important that staff members are able to bless and encourage great ministry ideas that originate outside themselves, and to guide those ideas toward the birth of new ministries. Behind almost every thriving ministry team in our church, one can find a staff member who serves as coach, cheerleader, and advocate.

Church staff members don't need detailed job descriptions so much as they need a grand purpose to be accomplished. They need a clear mandate from the church to advance the church's mission within a particular range of activity. The grander the purpose, the higher caliber of people a church can attract. For example, in the case of our new community recreation director position, we didn't make a laundry list of functions. We didn't prescribe when this person should be in the office or what leagues he should begin. We simply said we needed someone to lead us in building a community recreation ministry to serve 3,000 people a year. The biggest factor in the evaluation of our community recreation director is how many people are being included in that ministry. We measure not only total number of participants, however, but also look at the scope and breadth of the leadership teams who are doing the various recreational ministries. In most ministries, as the numbers of leaders increase, the numbers of participants will increase accordingly. In other words, the more leaders, the more impact! Dan Pezet, our rec director, could not begin to reach and serve 3,000 people with a hands-on style; that is, doing the ministries himself. It is not his job to coach, or even run any leagues. He has enlisted leaders to do all these things. If Dan chooses to coach a soccer team, he does this as a volunteer, for the sheer fun of it. Dan's job is to lead the leaders so that together they all accomplish what the recreation ministry needs to accomplish.

Leading the leaders means inviting, training, and carefully deploying persons into ministry based on their gifts. But leading leaders does not stop there. Leaders need to be coached on an ongoing basis. In large ministry divisions, the staff leader may choose to focus simply on *coaching the coaches,* who in turn coach and guide the people on the front lines of ministry. A coach helps to guide the leaders of a ministry around potential pitfalls. A coach helps leaders stay connected to the church's mission and values. A coach helps leaders discover resources to accomplish ministry: financial resources, people resources, curriculum resources, organizational resources, etc. Good coaches are often also cheerleaders, seeking to celebrate the victories won in order to encourage those who are in the trenches, delivering ministry.

Finally, staff members often need to function as advocates for ministry. Advocacy begins as we tell the stories of these ministry victories far and wide in the community. Such story telling raises the visibility of various ministries and increases their credibility. This, in turn, builds support in the church for these ministries, both in terms of financing and in terms of people signing on to join in the ministry. Advocacy also involves the communication of the ministry's vision and needs to people (both inside the main church leadership team and outside that team), so that resources might be channeled to the ministry.

All leaders, paid or not, should begin giving their ministry away from the moment that ministry commences. Pastors and music leaders tend to be among the worst "ministry hogs" in most churches. (Those who watch hogs eat will note their great eagerness for the task of eating but also a total lack of intent to share the food with others, or to even consider that others are trying to eat, too.) Any church staff position can be used as a platform for hogging the ministry, either through the attempt by the staff member to do it all alone, or through the attempt by the staff member to tightly control others who are doing ministry.

The reason pastors and musicians are so vulnerable to the temptation to hog the ministry and not to share it is because often these persons bring skills and training to the congregation that is not readily available within the congregation. They have often been to seminary. They reason to themselves that the church expects a high quality product that only they can deliver. This is sometimes half true; but only half true. Most pastors do not need to give away their preaching time, at least not in the short term. However, it is healthy for pastors to be coaching others who teach and preach from time to time, especially in smaller settings, apart from the main worship hours. Pastors should always be on the lookout for staff members and others who have raw gifts that, with nurturing, can grow to a very high level of skill.

In most places, ninety-nine percent of pastoral caring needs to be done by someone other than a paid pastor. Pastors need to mentor these caregivers in the congregation. Pastors in traditional congregations need to continue to deliver one percent of the caring, in high-profile ways, so that they retain credibility and integrity as servant leaders.

Most music leaders need to make some music themselves and not just administrate a music department. A music leader may continue to lead a high-profile worship team, and yet a dozen other music leaders and worship teams may spin out of the original team. Effective music leaders are constantly mentoring gifted people to lead vocal and instrumental groups.

For all paid staff positions, pastors included, we should measure effectiveness by total impact, by overall ministry results, and by leaders being developed. It is extremely counterproductive to evaluate staff based on how many things they do for the church. These devilish pieces of paper that we call job descriptions usually encourage staff members to busy themselves with three pages worth of prescribed activity. Many churches would profit from burning their job descriptions, and replacing them with one-paragraph profiles of the kinds of leaders that are needed and the broad results that should come from that leadership. This latter approach enables staff members to custom design their job around (1) the major goals to be accomplished, (2) the gifts of the staff member, and (3) the gifts of others on the teams that the staff member is coaching, all of which may be constantly changing. In other words, the staff member is empowered to do *whatever is expedient*, within the church's values, toward the achievement of specific and measurable results.

We pay staff members for two reasons. We pay them when we are looking for a high level of certain skills not readily available within the team of servants already present. And we pay them when we need more of their time and energy than they can afford to donate. People have a right and a responsibility to support themselves and their families financially. How much money that takes is an issue that has to be hammered out between each family and God. The church doesn't need to be in the business of deciding how much a person needs to be paid, or what size house they should be able to afford. However, there does need to be a group of leaders at the church that assesses how much the church is willing to pay to acquire excellent leadership. Hopefully, we can garner enough funding to underwrite a salary that will attract a leader we feel called to bring on board.

The Role of Unpaid Leadership

One difference between the church and business worlds is that the lion's share of the labor force doing ministry through the church is not paid, at least not in dollars and health benefits. The vast majority of leaders in a church find their financial support somewhere other than from the church. To take it one step further, the majority of leaders in a church, in truth, pay to work there. As tithers, they likely pay thousands of dollars a year to underwrite the church's work in addition to giving their time in ministry.

In thriving churches, the vast majority of ministry leaders and coaches are unpaid. Most of the ministry that happens is delivered by volunteers. In some churches, positions begin as volunteer and then transition to paid. At Gulf Breeze Church, the trend recently has been in the opposite direction. As we continue to discover and encourage the tremendous gifts that God has placed among our people, we have seen a couple of paid positions effectively filled by unpaid servant leaders.

In late 1999, we hired a full-time, East Campus-based Director of Multimedia Ministries. Essentially this person would oversee video production, computer networks, and worship audio-visuals. A few months later, the person we hired left for a better-paying job. However, by the time he left, a group of competent volunteers had risen up. Almost all of the sound and visual graphics for worship could now be produced by highly committed, unpaid leaders. The other components of that staff position were farmed out to other staff. As a result, payroll-related costs in the multimedia arena dropped for us during our first couple of years at the Community Life Center, even as we developed our multimedia ministry. I do not mean to infer that we will not someday move again to a full-time director in this area. But such a move will come only with a commitment to a major expansion in this ministry.

When we opened the Community Life Center, we provided a salaried assistant to the Director of Community Recreation. The programs could not have started so rapidly had we not given our director some staff help. However, within six months, we began phasing out the assistant position. The person we had hired as assistant felt called to another area of ministry in our church. We could have hired another assistant, but we elected not to do so, even as the rec program was exploding in scale. We chose this route because servant leaders began surfacing. In addition to the scores of servant leaders, the funds collected through registration fees allowed for the payment of league commissioners and various contract workers. Because of this, the amount of money going from the offering plate to the recreation ministry decreased in our first two years, even as the program grew.

This tremendous growth in unpaid servant leaders is certainly reducing the number of paid staff members we need per capita. Our church is growing, and so we are almost always increasing our paid staff. But we certainly operate more effectively with the added ministry of the unpaid staff than we would if we counted solely on the paid staff to do all the ministry.

The Most Important Quality in a Leader

There are at least five types of qualities that are important for leaders, both paid and unpaid. Training, experience, beliefs, relative giftedness, and attitude are all important issues. However the last quality on the list is, by far, the greatest of the five.

Attitude is more important than education, more important than experience, more important than purity of beliefs on all subjects theological, and more important than raw talent. It would be an overstatement to say that attitude is everything, because each of these other leadership components have a certain value. But attitude certainly impacts everything. A poor attitude can cancel out every component we have mentioned.

There is a sense in which the first four items are more outward than attitude. A person can clearly and simply quantify education, experience, and beliefs on a resume. Talent is also relatively obvious. Any number of references can vouch for a person's talent. Attitude, however, is a bit more elusive. It is inward. As I think about the role of this inner quality of the heart, I am reminded of what was said when Samuel anointed David, a kid with no resume, to be the king of Israel, "for the LORD does not see as mortals see; they look on the outward appearance, but the LORD looks on the heart." (1 Samuel 16:7b). This offers us a clue in discovering what is most important in making up a leader.

In terms of attitude in those who would be leaders among us, there are two key issues that we need to consider. First, a leader must buy in to the church's mission and values (and its core convictions of faith as well). Second, a leader must possess a servant's heart. Everything else should be somewhat negotiable.

Jeremy Morse, the Worship/Music Pastor at the Community Life Center, observed something about emerging worship leaders that I have not been able to shake. He said, "If a person, regardless of talent, can't play a supporting role in the worship band, we don't need to waste time putting them in a lead role." In other words, if there is lots of talent, lots of ego, but no servant heart, they don't belong in worship leadership. That same principle is true in every ministry area. A sense of servanthood is a prerequisite to leadership.

Many churches pay too much attention to educational degrees and certifications. The schools and organizations that offer various pedigrees very often do not understand the values and needs of post-Christendom churches. The best training for potential church leaders is to be mentored by a highly capable leader or ministry team. Some churches look for many years of previous ministry experience in their leaders. In a rapidly changing world, the amount of experience is actually less significant than the nature of the experience. The most valuable work experience may be outside the church altogether. The least valuable work experience may be ministry in a church with a significantly different congregational culture, or ministry in a church that functions as if it were still 1956. Too much emphasis on accumulated experience can skew the median age of a church's leadership too high, or can result in a church missing out on a capable twenty-something leader. Such a young leader just might, if given a chance, lead a church to reach for the stars and even touch a few. Some churches create too narrow a gate for leadership by demanding that all potential leaders sign a detailed statement of beliefs that moves far beyond core concepts and values. With each layer of criteria we place on our leaders, we shrink the circle of potential leaders.

A Moving Target

By the beginning of 1999, I had been assigned the task of directing the search for leadership for the Community Life Center. We were originally projected to open our doors by

June. Due to construction delays, this slid back to September. We were budgeted to begin bringing on the Community Life Center staff several months in advance of our grand opening, so that we could be ready to begin with a splash. Because we had so many positions to fill, our church's staff-parish relations committee set up a fast-track system of candidate searching and hiring in which no search committee was ever convened. Rather, they simply empowered me to write each job profile with input from appropriate leadership. Nationwide searches commenced for the Director of Community Recreation and the new Worship/Music Leader. In each case, I took personal responsibility for the search and worked with the staff-parish committee chairperson to convene a customized interview team for each position.

I began the year seeking to fill a different list of positions than what we actually ended up with twelve months later. We started with these positions on paper:

- Worship/Music pastor (overseeing East Campus worship services)
- Multimedia Technician (part-time)
- Director of Community Recreation
- Recreation Assistant (part-time)
- East Campus Director (part-time—overseeing facility administration)
- East Campus Administrative Assistant
- Facilities Maintenance

A couple of these positions were combined with positions already in existence to make up full-time jobs. Counting myself, this plan looked for six and a quarter staff persons (in full-time equivalency) at the Community Life Center in addition to preschool staff and some hourly positions funded through recreation user fees.

Two years later, the list had expanded to look like this:

- Worship/Music Pastor (also now overseeing Multi-media ministry teams)
- *Multimedia Technician POSITION ELIMINATED*
- Director of Community Recreation
- *Recreation Assistant POSITION ELIMINATED*
- Welcome Desk Director NEW
- Welcome Desk hourly staff (part-time)
- Director of Hospitality and Single Adult Ministries (instead of East Campus Director)
- Children's Ministries Associate NEW
- East Campus Administrative Assistant
- Facilities Maintenance Supervisor
- Facilities Assistant (full-time) NEW
- *Director of Multimedia Ministries POSITION CREATED LATE 1999, THEN ELIMINATED*
- *Community Leader for Youth and Young Adults POSI-TION CREATED IN 2000, THEN MOVED TO MAIN CAMPUS*

Why did the list of positions change so much over two years?

1. We hired great people and then designed their responsibilities around their gifts, rather than confining them to arbitrary job descriptions.
2. Our plans for the East Campus proved to be more ambitious than what we could accomplish with a smaller staff.
3. As the completion of construction slid from a spring date to a fall date, we were left with roughly eight months of budgeted funding for East Campus staff in 1999, which we would now use over a shorter period of time. This enabled us to hire more staff for the last half of 1999. We believed that we were hiring extraordinary people who would pay for themselves by 2000. And indeed, when stewardship pledges came in for 2000, the increase was such that every position we had added late in 1999 was easily funded for the following year.

4. Throughout 1999, our church operated with a steadily growing surplus in our Ministry Budget account. This was due to the conservative manner in which we budget. (We collect pledges and then build a budget based on pledges.) The resulting surplus in 1999 was greater than usual, further enhancing our ability to hire additional staff, as well as to pay for unbudgeted ministry start-up needs. If you think of ministry as a wildfire, these surplus funds enabled us to pour gasoline on the wildfire at just the right time. Without such surplus funds, we could not have added staff as aggressively, or even purchased the land so quickly two years earlier. Conservative budgeting has continually provided the positive cash flow that enables us to respond to needs as they arise and seize opportunities quickly.

5. Finally, during the year 2000, some areas became less dependent on staff, enabling us to shift staff resources to other areas where additional help was needed. Staff dollars needed in maturing ministries (such as multimedia) were shrinking, where unpaid servant leaders were rising up, allowing those funds to become available in other areas, like staffing the Welcome Desk.

During 1999, the number of pastors and ministry directors on staff at Gulf Breeze United Methodist Church increased from ten to sixteen. When one considers this along with the fact that we added a major worship service at a new location, it is no wonder that our fall 1999 worship attendance was consistently up between three and four hundred per Sunday as compared to the same day the previous year.

How Many Paid Staff Do We Need?

Historically, Gulf Breeze Church has been understaffed. The size of our pastor/director staff has been consistently smaller than what is typically needed for a church of our size. (We do not count administrative staff, secretaries, custodians, and technicians as pastor/director staff.) Here is the size of our pastor/director staff relative to our average worship attendance at various points during the past decade.

Year	Worship attendance	Staff needed*	Size of our staff
1991	950	10	5
1993	1,150	12	5.5
1995	1,280	13	6.75
1997	1,320	14	8
1998	1,400	14	10
1999	1,600	16	15
2000	1,750	18	16
2001	1,900	19	18

Standard wisdom through the 1990s for churches with centralized program ministries (such as music, youth, recreation, etc.) was that one pastor/director was needed for every 100 in worship attendance, if a church was to be staffed for growth. These recommended ratios continue to be relevant.

One could conclude, based upon the above data, that under-staffing was as much a factor in our church's plateaued growth in the mid-90s as was lack of space at our Main Campus. For three years (1995, 1996, and 1997) our attendance hovered around 1,300. However, by 1998, even though we had no additional space, we were clearly growing again. During 1999, our attendance averaged about 1,500 prior to the East Campus Grand Opening, without additional space. When we made the decision to develop the East Campus, we assumed that our growth would be negligible until fall of 1999. We were surprised that our growth accelerated during this two-year preparation for the expansion. It seems very likely that the increase in our staff size between 1997 and 1999 was a key factor in this growth. Then, once the new campus opened, attendance skyrocketed. And we were ready—staffed to serve and incorporate the masses of people who came into our church's life during late 1999 and 2000.

By phasing in the new positions at different points during the year, the total financial impact of the 1999 staff expansion was spread between two fiscal years. We were able to keep our church-wide personnel costs at no more than fifty-two percent of our annual church ministry budget. In addition, we added this staff as a part of a larger plan through which we knew that we would experience a growth spurt. We counted on the growth spurt to help pay for the increased costs in the years 2000 and beyond.

There may be situations where a church anticipates a need to add staff that pushes the church's personnel expenses beyond sixty percent of its budget. In such cases, the first two years of a new staff position can be funded by means of a special fund drive. When churches conduct capital fund campaigns for building expansion, they can set aside a portion of the fund to pay for start-up personnel and operational expenses in the new facility. They can set forth a budget and a plan so that by the third year in the new facility, the ministry and the staff are paying for themselves. Personally, I would choose to designate part of a capital fund for staff expense only if I could see clearly that the new position would create enough church growth to pay for itself within a couple years. In our case, both our director of community recreation position and our worship/music pastor position were the kinds of staff additions that did this.

A well-executed capital fund drive embraces a cause that people can get their hearts around. With professional assistance, such a fund drive can be expected to yield twice the church's regular annual income over a period of three years. For example, if a church has an annual budget of $200,000, they are probably capable of raising an additional $400,000, spread over three years, at about $133,000 each year. If just twenty percent of the $400,000 was set aside for strategic staffing expansion, that would yield an additional

$80,000 for new staff salaries over the same three year period. Churches should be careful not to assume that they cannot afford the kinds of capable staff necessary for major ministry expansion.

Great Leaders Are Attracted to Great Projects

The best things we had to offer prospective staff were (1) the opportunity to be a part of something extraordinary, and to make a name for themselves in their field; (2) the opportunity to live and settle in a beautiful coastal community; and (3) the promise that *as the ministry grew*, the church would seek to take care of them and keep them for a long time. Because we have been in a growth mode, our church has never been in a position to woo world-class staff with money. So we woo them with what we can find.

Where a church does not have as attractive a community setting to offer potential staff and their families, the more important it is to offer them the opportunity to be part of something extraordinary! In *Built to Last*, James Collins and Jerry Porras coined the term "big, hairy, audacious goals," known in shorthand as BHAG's. They demonstrate how organizations that possess huge goals typically surpass comparable organizations in their growth and scope of influence. Great leaders are attracted to such organizations. In case after case, Gulf Breeze Church has attracted extraordinary staff because we were attempting something great for God. Nineteenth-century ministry pioneer William Carey said, "Attempt great things for God; expect great things from God." Churches that exude this kind of spirit seldom have difficulty finding the caliber of people they need to achieve great things for God. BHAG's attract great staff.

BHAG's also encourage certain present staff to relocate to a less ambitious, less frenzied place of ministry. During the two years that our church transitioned from one campus to two, we experienced a total turnover in staff in our children's ministries division, lost two youth ministry associates, and two consecutive directors of our single adult ministries. On the support staff side, we lost all our custodians and several secretaries. Several of these people who left were extraordinarily competent Christian servants. The role of staff was changing, however, and not everyone was energized by the new dynamics. Our experience in staff turnover during 1998-99 brings to mind a very pointed statement John Maxwell made to the staff of Skyline Wesleyan Church in San Diego several years ago, shortly after he became pastor there. He said, "What I know about you is that you have what it takes to build a church to a thousand. What I don't know is whether or not you have what it takes to build a church to two thousand." He says that one year later, only three persons from the original staff remained.

This principle about great leaders being drawn to great projects is also true of unpaid leadership. In too many churches, the best talent sits out the game on the sidelines because they perceive their church's goals to be less than inspirational. I am continually amazed by the varied talents represented in our church and in the wider community, by the number of people who have achieved the extraordinary in their professional lives. The Community Life Center project shook quite a few such leaders out of the bushes, people with great talent who were around all along, but whose talents were never engaged before.

Searching the World Over

I share the following in order for you to catch a sense of both the chaos of the search for staff, and the way that God brings order to the chaos. Please note the absence of the traditional search committee composed of representatives from various factions in the church, starting with a job description and then looking for a person to fill it.

A search is much easier to conduct with one or two people in charge of it. Then, once there are two or three top candidates, an interview team of four to six people is assembled, partly of staff and partly of others who know something about the skills and gifts necessary for the position. Ideally, the interview team interviews the top candidates on the same day, then makes a recommendation to the personnel committee or whomever officially hires staff at that particular church. They can recommend that the church pass on all three and keep fishing, or that they proceed to cut a deal with one of those interviewed. Here is what this whole process looked like for us as we gathered staff leadership for the Community Life Center:

Nine months prior to our grand opening, the two positions that were uppermost in our focus were the Worship/Music Pastor and the Director of Community Recreation. During the fall of 1998, I had begun a nationwide search for both, putting out some ads and accumulating two files of possible candidates. The salaries that I had to offer were modest for both positions. Thus, the profile of the new staff member we would likely attract was somebody young, talented, and looking for their "big break."

I knew that the first position was especially critical. Quality, contemporary Christian music is essential to the successful planting of most new worship services. Bill Easum told me in December 1998 that I was "behind the eight ball" on this search. Because this person would need adequate start-up time in Gulf Breeze prior to fall, and because they might need time to wrap up present commitments before coming to Gulf Breeze, it became urgent that we identify and cut a deal with our new worship pastor in the first quarter of the year.

I found only a handful of viable candidates for worship pastor who (1) were capable of the task, (2) would be comfortable with our church's personality, and (3) would be able to function effectively in our community culture. I networked in every direction I could think of. Len Wilson, from Ginghamsburg Church in Tipp City, Ohio, told me that our position description was flawed in combining both music ministry and multimedia ministry oversight in one position. He said that to combine both of those things in one person would create a monster that I did not want to meet. He encouraged me to find somebody who was competent in one or the other discipline. The trouble was that we didn't have the money for both.

By January, I had five decent candidates. That was it. One had come to me via a posting at a prominent music ministry website. Another had come via a posting in our denominational newspaper. The third came from a posting on the Willow Creek Association's website. We found the final two through networking. Of these latter candidates, one was unable to relocate due to his green card status (he was British) and the other prayed about it but could find no sense of release from his present ministry position.

I traveled to Dallas in early January and combed north central Texas for leads (simply an area that I know well with a lot of competent folks in ministry). One of the places I visited while in Texas was University Baptist Church in Waco, a church that rose to national prominence in the 1990s as part of a new wave of young adult-led churches. I was deeply moved by the worship service I attended at UBC on January 10, 1999. On Tuesday of that week, I traveled back to Waco in search of a young man in the UBC band who came highly recommended by their pastors as one of the most promising leaders among their graduating seniors. Once in Waco, I called from a pay phone and found Ben Dudley at home putting a frozen lasagna in the oven for lunch. He immediately changed his lunch plans and we spent a couple of hours together, during which I realized I had found the first East Campus staff member. Ben wasn't the person to be worship pastor, but I saw immediately that he was the kind of person we were looking for. I knew we needed him. He was twenty-two years old and his eyes lit up as he heard what we were trying to do.

Now, why would a church want to offer a position to a person they didn't officially have a job for, even before they had filled any of the positions they were funded to fill? Because:

1. The person is simply so right for the church—he/she is immediately able to catch the vision of what the church is seeking to do.
2. The person has been nurtured by another extraordinary church. (In Ben's case, he had been nurtured by two extraordinary churches, one a flagship of progressive ministry in a traditional setting and the other, a church on the cutting edge of ministry to young adults. He would bring values to us from both places.)
3. The person has a combination of gifts that the church needs badly in its next generation of leadership. (In Ben's case, he was a recreation major. And we were going into the recreation business big-time. He was also an excellent musician. And we needed excellent musicians.)
4. The Spirit of God says, "Get this person! You need them on your team."

Ben needed a place to do his recreation internship in the fall of 1999 in order to graduate from college. So I promised him an internship, taking what would have been a half-time recreation assistant salary over eight months and stacking it all into four months as a full-time position. I offered him this position as a four-month internship, during which time he could get to know us and we could get to know him. I had no guarantee that we would have a full-time position available for him beyond fall 1999. However, I believed that God had led me to Ben. And I trusted that God would make a way for us to retain him beyond his internship, if God wanted Ben to be an ongoing part of our ministry team. In addition to his work as recreation assistant, I figured Ben would be helpful in the establishment of our East Campus worship band.

In one respect, the way I hired Ben was a textbook case in how *not* to hire staff. Both with respect to his music ministry and his recreation leadership, I was promising him a place assisting leaders that we had not even identified yet. It is a basic principle that you hire department heads first, and then allow department heads to build their own teams. In another sense, the way Ben came to us is a textbook case demonstrating the fact that there are no hard-and-fast rules anymore in hiring staff. Because there was only a four-month commitment involved, there was no need to even convene an interview team on Ben. He and I just cut a deal face to face. A church can give its senior staff latitude to do such things, so long as they know where the money will come from in the personnel budget. I knew how to pay Ben for four months. After that, I had no idea.

Back to the main search at hand; I still needed a worship/music pastor. By February, two of the five candidates had fallen off the list due to factors outside my control. Of the three remaining, only one was still a viable candidate in my mind after extensive reference checks and phone interviews between the candidates and The Gallup Organization in Lincoln, Nebraska. (Gallup provides a good leadership assessment for potential church staff members. This has been helpful to us in numerous staff searches.) The only candidate still standing by the first of February was a Canadian with an outstanding ministry track record and a sincere interest in our position. We had visited several times on the phone and really connected each time. The Florida panhandle is, however, a long way from British Columbia, and the cultural chasm remained a major concern for both of us.

We decided we would bring this candidate in to interview. However, our church has a policy of seeking to interview at least two people, on the same day if possible. I had to find a second candidate very quickly. But after more than two months of looking, I had found very little.

Having exhausted all my leads, I decided one afternoon to jump on the World Wide Web and email campus ministers at various universities around the nation. I knew that some of the larger campus ministries had become hotbeds of cutting-edge creativity in worship music. From the approximately twenty campus ministries that I contacted, I received two replies. One was from a potential candidate at Mississippi State who wrote to ask, "Who are you and how did you get my name?" The other was from Enoch Hendry, the United Methodist campus pastor at University of Tennessee, Knoxville. Enoch felt he knew just the right person to help us launch our new worship community. His name was Jeremy Morse.

Jeremy was serving as a pastor of a storefront church in Knoxville. We had a great conversation on the phone. But after sleeping on the idea, Jeremy sensed that he needed to stay where he was and emailed me a note to this effect. Throughout 1999, Gulf Breeze Church had server problems which interfered with incoming and outgoing email. Twice, Jeremy's email to me was returned to him. His *"Dear Paul"* letter couldn't get through. Meanwhile that same week, a string of events led him to change his mind. He decided he had better talk to us. So we flew him down to interview along with the other candidate. The day after Jeremy agreed to come interview, his third attempt at the "thanks but no thanks" email finally came through.

When we interviewed, Jeremy demonstrated considerably less experience than the other candidate. The other candidate had experience running a huge and complex music ministry. Jeremy did not. But Jeremy understood and embraced the vision of what we were seeking to do.

Jeremy was the only seminary graduate who came on our East Campus team that first year, other than myself. His degree, from Princeton, did not help him get this job. I was more encouraged by his statement, in the interview process, that he had needed to unlearn most of what he was taught in seminary during his first five years out of school.

Some might assume that the lack of seminary training for most of our staff might result in theological ineptitude or naivete. However, I have not found seminary experience to be a significant predictor of theological position or of the ability to think theologically. Our staff come from a variety of theological positions, give indication of high intelligence, and are highly gifted for their respective ministries.

The community recreation director search produced two dozen solid applicants. They came from responses to two ads we ran, one in a denominational newspaper and the other in a recreational trade journal. There were also a handful of excellent local people whom we considered.

When it came down to the final two, it was between the assistant director of an outstanding community recreation ministry in a 6,000-member church and a young man who had never directed a church recreation ministry but who had excelled in setting up a sixteen-site program working with YMCA.

This latter candidate, Dan Pezet, had also done an internship with Disney World as part of his bachelor's degree at the University of Florida. He had internalized Disney's approach to hospitality (one of our core values). Up until the week before he moved to Gulf Breeze in May 1999, Dan was the voice of welcome at the *Bug's Life* show at Disney's Animal Kingdom. More than any other staff candidate we interviewed, Dan possessed the vision of what we were seeking to do with the Community Life Center. He joined our staff just prior to his twenty-fifth birthday.

None of these first three hires had ever done before what we would be asking them to do. In this sense, some might say we took a risk with each. In each case, they were simply very impressive young leaders who were powerfully engaged by the vision of our church. They were each drawn to us, and we to them, because they believed, *really believed*, in what we were doing as a church. Two of the three were chosen over another candidate with significantly more experience. We hired for attitude, vision, and personhood. We looked at training, experience, and theological stance only insofar as those things offered a glimpse of what they might become. The bottom line was that each of the persons we hired had a special energy for the work before them, a sense of calling, and a deep desire to be in *this* place in *this* time doing *this* work. Admittedly, they were and are a tremendously talented group. But the secret of their success lies deeper than their outward talents. The secret is in their hearts. I fully believe they came from God, each of them.

Right Under Our Noses

All our other leaders, both paid and unpaid, came from our local community, many from beyond our church membership. In each case, the number one criteria in those who have thrived in the work has been that their heart was in this ministry. From our building maintenance staff to our Welcome Desk Coordinator, who leads our front line of communication on the phone and in the lobby, each of the people who are part of our leadership team have been sent straight from God. Their stories are heart-warming. They don't get up each morning to go to a job. They get up to do God's work. Every last one of them. I consider myself to be a creative headhunter, but I cannot take credit for this team. I can see in hindsight that what we did to advertise and to network was far less significant than what God did in bringing this group of people together.

Our Director of Single Adult Ministries, Anita Sharron, came to Christ the day she first walked in to Gulf Breeze Church, twenty years ago. She came on board our staff in 1999 to bring healing to our single adult ministry. Quickly, we saw her gift of hospitality and her passion for the community. We moved her office to the Community Life Center and placed her in charge of hospitality and welcoming, in addition to her leadership with single adults. Anita's warmth and love has made an enormous impact in creating a welcoming atmosphere at the East Campus. Here was a person who believed deeply in the mission long before she ever thought about becoming part of our staff.

As we began to share the vision with our congregation in the summer of 1999 about the new worship service that was soon to begin, several people stepped forth to help. One of those people was Jonathan Muldoon, a twenty-eight-year-old adjunct English instructor at the University of West Florida. We soon discovered his experience in computers and video editing. Before the year was out, Jonathan was a full-time member of our staff. As a new Christian, he offered a valuable perspective as one of the key collaborators in the design of the new worship service. He led in the production of several major video pieces, including the "Are You Having Fun Yet?" video that ran for a month on local cable TV and introduced the Community Life Center to thousands of people. When Jonathan left our staff a few months later, there were others who filled the gaps he left. The wonderful thing about multimedia ministry is that it engages people who may never have been able to use their gifts at church before. Most communities these days are overflowing with technologically gifted people who will be drawn to churches attempting to do high-tech things for God.

Before the Community Life Center was ever built, Sandy Gutting had a dream of such a place. Once we opened, Sandy found us, began attending worship, experienced a life transformation, was baptized, and became active in a couple of our hospitality ministries. In the fall of 2000, her job came to an end as the business where she had worked for thirteen years was sold. That very week, we found funding to create a position we call Welcome Desk Coordinator. This person is the front line of communication for thousands of people who call in or who walk into our lobby, and is also responsible for overseeing a team of others who cover that desk eighty hours a week. For most folks, their first contact with the Community Life Center is their contact with the Welcome Desk. The day Sandy Gutting took over the Welcome Desk ministry was the day most of our communication and public relations difficulties ended. Every time I see her there, I say a prayer of thanks. She had a vision of the place even before Gulf Breeze Church did. God was getting her ready for ministry. If any one position on our team could be singled out as the most critical, it would be what Sandy does for us.

For all the people we reached in our first year, had Sandy been there, we would have reached many more. Too many times, the phone rang forever before it was answered, or simply switched to voice mail. Too many times, messages were lost. Too many times, volunteers did not have the information they needed at their fingertips to answer questions from the public. If I had it to do over again, I would be willing to cut something else in order to start with a world-class leader at the Welcome Desk. This is one area where we really could have done better from Day One. Nevertheless, God supplied the leader locally, at the very moment we were ready.

Interviewing and Hiring

I feel a tremendous sense of gratitude to Darryl Lapointe, who chaired our staff-parish relations committee during these critical years of transition to a multiple campus ministry. Darryl's leadership pushed us eons ahead in personnel administration in only a matter of months. Darryl is CEO of a local firm that owns and manages a string of hotels. In 1994, Darryl's only experience with our church was jogging past all the Sunday morning hubbub each week. One day he dared to come in. Soon he experienced a life transformation. He joined the church by profession of his faith. He enrolled in a weekly Bible study group. Within a couple years, he agreed to offer his business expertise to our church as he joined our staff-parish relations committee.

Under Darryl Lapointe's leadership, the following practices were implemented:

1. We began to use an employee leasing firm with our lay staff, effectively removing untold hours of payroll administration out of the church financial office. This

also enabled us to offer more benefits to our staff per benefit dollar spent.

2. The committee shifted its attention from micro issues to macro issues, setting broad policies, and allowing senior staff to evaluate and supervise the other staff without direct committee involvement.

3. The search process for new staff was delegated to the staff member who would serve as supervisor. That staff member would write the preliminary job profile on the position being filled and find candidates in any way that he/she chose.

4. Interview teams were chaired by the staff member conducting the search. A staff-parish committee member was appointed by the chairperson to serve on the team plus a couple other persons, chosen for their investment in the ministry area in question and/or their expertise in a discipline relevant to the position being filled.

If a church chooses to take such an approach, I would recommend that the senior pastor be a part of every interview team for new pastors and ministry directors for a couple of years at least. This enables the senior pastor to have ownership in the decision. As time passes, the staff grows, and the senior staff becomes more comfortable with this process, the senior pastor may become selective in the interviews he/she attends.

Our standard interview process is now as follows:

1. We try to bring in at least two people, preferably three, to interview on the same day, each of whom honestly could be "the one." We try not to interview until we have a race between at least two strong candidates. Three is better than two for several reasons. Three choices are less likely to polarize an interview team. Sometimes when only two competent persons are compared, one candidate will not stand out as a clear choice. Add a third point of comparison, and it will often become clearer which one is the right choice. We

don't bring in a third, however, unless all three have an honest shot at the position.

2. Each interview lasts one hour. The candidate's resume and any other relevant material is given to the interview team members by mail a few days prior to the interview. During the first twenty minutes, only the chair of the interview team (usually the supervising staff member) asks questions. Everyone else listens. Questions are open-ended, so that the candidate will talk and talk. At the twenty-minute mark, the candidate is excused from the room so that the team can compare observations and concerns. A further line of questioning is developed. At the thirty-minute mark, the candidate returns and the interview continues, with the chair of the team asking all questions until the fifty-minute mark. At this point, he/she opens up the floor to the rest of the team for any follow-up questions we may wish to ask.

3. After completing the three interviews, the interview team checks to see if they have sufficient consensus around one of the candidates to offer a job. If sufficient consensus does not exist, the team agrees to a course of action. We may send a couple of people to observe the candidate in action in their present ministry setting. We may assign additional questions to the candidate to be answered in writing or in a subsequent interview. In our 1999 search for our recreation director, we had a tie. Both candidates were simply outstanding, so the interview team agreed to pray about it, and then I polled them by phone. They still felt good with both candidates, though we could only hire one. Finally, they just said, "Paul, you are the one who has to work with the guy. Make a call." So I did.

This interview style enables us to keep our focus and avoid chasing rabbits in the interview. A bad interview process can scare off an outstanding staff prospect. On the other hand, when a candidate is struggling in the interview, certain persons on the interview team may instinctively wish to change the subject or help the candidate out. Our process keeps the committee members quiet, so that they do not inadvertently obscure the learning that is happening about the person being interviewed. As painful as it is to watch a person blow an interview, it is so much better that they fail in an interview than to fail in the job after relocating their family and establishing a network of personal relationships in the church.

Lines of Accountability

It is important that there be direct accountability between church employees and their respective supervisors. The less interference there is by a personnel committee in the day-to-day operation of the ministry team, the better! Personnel committees need to empower senior staff to make decisions and to supervise the other staff. At times, the senior staff may wish to turn to a personnel committee, or to certain members of such a body, for counsel. Certain decisions are best shared by senior staff and a personnel committee operating in prayerful consensus. Other times, the personnel committee can simply empower the staff to hire and terminate employees. At least one, possibly two or three, senior staff members may be accountable directly to the personnel body or central leadership team.

With unpaid leadership, accountability may seem a bit more fuzzy. In a permission-giving environment, we try to say to all the people in the church, "Go and do ministry, be creative, be pro-active. Advance the mission. Uphold the values. And have fun! You don't need approval beforehand." In such cases, ministry happens sort of the way a family takes a vacation. They are free to go north, south, east, or west, to stay in nice hotels or to pitch a tent alongside the road, to eat peanut butter sandwiches or to enjoy five-star restaurants. They simply have to mind the rules of the road. If they do not mind the rules of the road, the flashing lights appear in the rearview mirror, as has happened more than once when my family has been on vacation. The flashing lights mean, usually, that I have exceeded the local speed limit, that I have strayed outside the road rules. The flashing lights are a means of accountability. Such accountability can exist without asking people to file route plans with the highway patrol.

Too many great ministries never are birthed because people do not have the energy to seek the permission of some central committee in their church. Most prevailing churches today do not seek to control ministry, but simply provide (with the mission and values) a framework within which their people are free to innovate and create great ministry. When there is a problem, the flashing lights appear. In my experience, there is so rarely a problem that the flashing lights go mostly unused. In each case, we try to link up each ministry with a designated leader, paid or unpaid, who can serve as a coach and an encourager to that ministry team. This designated leader offers feedback as needed. Where the ministry team requests funding from general church sources, this designated leader serves as that team's advocate in church budget planning.

Many growing ministries may have funding streams apart from the central church budget. These streams of funding include user fees, monetary donations to that particular ministry, and grants from outside the church. When a ministry area establishes an ongoing dependence on the central church budget for funding, an additional line of accountability is assured.

The Challenges of Multiple Sites

The most critical issue for the staff of a multiple-site church is the relationship between the lead pastors at the various sites. Had Herb Sadler and I not been on the same page with respect to vision, priorities, and even theology, the move to two campuses could have been a disaster. Herb and I have different personalities, different gifts, and somewhat different preaching styles. And yet there is a deep reservoir of mutual friendship and respect that exists between us. There must be unity between the pastors of a multi-site church. Period. There must be unity between the pastors of a single-site church where more than one pastor preaches each Sunday.

I am often asked if the two-campus approach works. The answer is always "Yes, so long as Herb and I get along." The day we don't is the day we will have a mess on our hands.

For churches seeking to move beyond the senior pastor/associate pastor model to simply a team of pastors, it is probably easier to have three, rather than two, in charge. If two people get into a rift, they can divide a church. If two hit a snag in a threesome, the third pastor will often work to reestablish a sense of consensus, or, at the very least, offer a tie-breaking vote. When the members of such a team emerge from behind closed doors, they must always emerge united. Our church moved to a team pastor model in April 2001 when Mack Strange joined our pastoral team. Herb, Mack, and I began serving as three co-pastors of one church on two campuses.

Our staffs from both campuses gather every other Tuesday morning, usually at the Main Campus, for a staff meeting. The meeting lasts ninety minutes, including worship time. Various team meetings may follow this meeting, including the convening of the East Campus staff alone to deal with issues not relevant to the larger group. During the first few months of our life as a multi-site congregation, when we lacked inter-office email between our two sites, we needed a weekly staff meeting to hold us all together. As solid communication lines have developed between sites, we have been able to reduce the number of staff meetings by half.

One of the ways we have unified our staff and our campuses has been to ask most of our ministry directors to oversee ministry on both sites. Because of this practice, very few staff members think of themselves as purely East Campus or Main Campus people. They see both campuses as venues where they lead in ministry. The most obvious exception to this approach has been in the area of music ministry. There are two separate, but complementary, music ministry umbrellas, one based at each site. We did this primarily so that there would be a strong link between the worship leader and the primary teaching/preaching pastor at each location.

By our grand opening weekend in fall of 1999, despite the stress of wondering if the toilets would flush, I was amazed at how relaxed I was, especially in comparison with eight months earlier. In February, it had all been on my shoulders, and I knew that I had to find the key staff leaders for things to happen as they should. But by September, I felt as if the key battles had already been won. There were now many shoulders to share the load. We had a great facility and great crowd. We had a great team of leaders. I was able to look at these leaders and to breathe a sigh of relief, even before the doors ever officially opened. Whatever happened in the weeks ahead, it was bound to be good.

CHAPTER SIX

Taking Christian Worship to the Community

Recently, I was traveling with friends in a nearby city. I wanted to show them the interior of a historic old sanctuary. When we arrived, a worship service was about to begin. There was a sign posted near the front door which read as follows:

VISITORS DO NOT ENTER

RELIGIOUS SERVICES IN PROGRESS

PLEASE RETURN LATER

Here was a church whose visitors consisted mostly of tourists who came to see the architecture. The church assumed that none of these guests would wish to stay and join in the worship of God. Though this church's doors are open seven days a week to the public, they are not open with any sense of expectancy that those who come through their doors will choose to share in their spiritual community.

Most churches do not post actual "Keep Out" signs. But in tiny ways, even the most community-oriented of churches can communicate that worship is for insiders, not for everyone. When worship is so antiquated in form that ordinary people in our communities can make little sense of it, we are communicating a similar message.

WORSHIP IS FOR US

IT IS NOT FOR YOU

COME BACK LATER

Thankfully, a powerful consensus is emerging in churches across North America that Christian worship must change in some key ways order to stay in touch with the persons we are seeking to lead into God's presence. Many of these changes can be offered in new services, so that those who are comfortable with the status quo can keep "their service" free of sweeping changes in music and style. It has been proven over and again that the most constructive way for most churches to move forward in worship is to move toward multiple services and multiple styles. This enables the new services to develop freely without constant road blocks thrown up due to the discomfort of long-time church members. This tactic also allows these members to support progressive change without our antagonizing them and inadvertently alienating them from our mission.

Let's Set the Alarm for 4:30

To really understand where I am coming from on Sunday mornings as a pastor, first you would need to get up with me at 4:30 A.M. The quiet time between my first cup of coffee and around 7:00 A.M. on Sundays is my favorite time of the week. My sermon is already planned, and yet there is a sense in which, at 5:00 A.M. on Sundays, it is still just a bunch of words on paper. In the next two hours, though, those words come to life in me. And often as they come to life, the words begin to change and to dance far away from anything I wrote down earlier in the week. I find in this early morning time that I am energized with expectancy about the service. I was not always this way. This time became fun for me once I gave up my heavy dependency on sermon notes. Each Sunday morning, I let go of sermon notes, except for some key words on post-it notes, placed strategically on the pages of my Bible. The whole experience is akin to the feeling I had many years ago when I discarded the training wheels from my bicycle. I come away from this early morning time with a sense that God and I are in this thing together, believing that the most powerful moments of spiritual connection in that morning's worship service(s) will likely be related to things that were not in our worship team's planned script. For me, early Sunday morning is about linking hands with God for the work before us that day. Because leading worship is my work, there is a sense in which my most significant personal experience of worship on Sunday happens before the sun comes up, as God and I get ready.

The other thing you need to know about me is that from 6:00 to 7:00 A.M. on Sundays, during the latter portion of this holy time, I listen to a National Public Radio program entitled "With Heart and Voice," which features classical church music, largely pipe organ and choirs from cathedrals around the world. I love that show. I am off-balance when I miss it. I listen to this radio show with my Bible open to my preaching text for the morning, mentally tuning in and out on the music, as I work through what God is trying to say to me and through me that morning.

Three hours later I will be leading worship dressed in a golf shirt and standing alongside a rock band.

Now, why do I tell you all this? Every preacher has his or her Sunday morning routine. None is necessarily superior to another. I share the above information to reveal the source of two powerful tensions within me as a worship leader.

The first is the tension between planning and spontaneity. I never travel without a map and a plan. But my feeling about maps and plans is that they are there for the moment when all else fails. Experience has taught me that often the most special moments in a trip come by surprise, often with sudden alterations to the itinerary. The same is true in leading worship. I have taken the Myers Briggs Inventory several times over the years, and each time it tells me that I am, by nature, a planner. Spontaneity is not my native language. And yet I need both planning and spontaneity in order to give God my best on Sunday mornings. I need to do my homework, but I also need to cultivate a sense of trust in God's presence and work in me, with me, and often, in spite of me. Another worship leader may prefer spontaneity. Planning will not be their native language. It is just as important for such leaders to learn to do their homework each week as it is for me to learn to be spontaneous on Sunday mornings.

The second tension in me as a worship leader is between church and the broader culture, between the two villages we discussed in chapter one. I think a lot of folks, especially from outside our church, see me innovating in worship and they assume that I am detached from Christian tradition. What they don't realize is that my soul is refreshed each Sunday by the sounds of a pipe organ, as I listen to the sounds of Mass at Notre Dame. I've been attending church on Sundays since I was two-weeks old. I feel a very powerful sense of connection to mainstream Christian heritage and to a wide range of traditions of the worldwide Christian community. I feel at home in both evangelical and more liberal churches. I have yet to find a church where I cannot worship. My world is pretty big. I do what I do where God has placed me with an awareness that I am a part of something way bigger than simply leading an indigenous worship service in a Florida coastal community.

However, I am also an evangelist at heart. If I had to choose between the style of music and worship forms that best met my own needs and a more culturally indigenous approach that reached the people God has sent me to serve, it would be an easy decision for me. The spiritual needs of unchurched people are going to prevail for me every time.

The way I would lead worship on U.S. 98 in Gulf Breeze, Florida, looks different from how I would lead worship in rural upstate New York, or how I would lead worship with young professionals in uptown Chicago.

I sense that many worship traditionalists think that the tremendous insurgence of non-traditional worship forms somehow reflects hostility towards tradition. While I cannot speak for other pastors leading non-traditional worship services, I can say that our team has carefully chosen worship forms that are unconventional, not because we harbor any hostility towards tradition, but simply because we want to reach the people God has placed in our neighborhood, many of whom are not responding to more traditional approaches.

It has nothing whatsoever to do with what I like and don't like. It's not about me; it's about God. It's about the people in Gulf Breeze, Florida, that God wants to gather and to reach. I remain part of a church that is committed both to innovative worship forms and to more traditional forms of worship, complete with hymn books, vestments, and creeds.

What Has to Happen to Call It Worship?

Connection between people and God is the point of worship. Worship is a coming together to experience God, in the hope that the experience will transform our lives in some way. We now have many centuries of accumulated worship experience from which to draw as we seek to design and lead worship that is effective in helping people make this critical connection with God. It makes sense to pay attention to what has worked in the past—to lead people to the streams where past generations have been known to get a drink. It also makes sense to pay attention to the needs of the people we are seeking to lead in worship, taking their life issues seriously, and inviting their input into the planning and evaluation of what we call worship.

Worship is a two-way street—reaching out with the people to God and reaching toward the people on behalf of God. Worship leaders, along with every media we employ to lead worship, sit squarely in the middle of this two-way street. Because God is reaching out to us in worship, and reaching through those of us who lead in worship, I have often made the statement that Christian worship is evangelism. I know this statement bothers certain people. There are purists who feel that this taints worship with a pragmatic motive. However, I am unable to imagine worshiping the God revealed in Christ without this experience drawing us toward that God. Even the great Cathedrals of Christendom draw the worshiper's attention upwards. In this sense, these ancient places of worship are evangelistic. If I walked into a cathedral and the setting did not lift my soul but depressed or confused me, that building would, for me, be a poor setting for worship. There are many dark, isolated fortress-type churches, where local people would never want to go and worship. These buildings, which may have invited people to an experience of God in another day, may have outlived their usefulness as houses of worship. There are pieces of music that may have caused spirits to soar two hundred years ago, and which, in select locations, might still have that effect on the people gathered in worship. To others, however, these same musical pieces may seem odd and meaningless. This is why we need to worship with a variety of music that reflects the unique and indigenous cultures of the people in each place. No matter how fine the sermon, how rehearsed and refined the music, no matter how brilliant the stained glass, if people are gathering and not connecting with God, something is wrong.

The New Testament record is remarkably simple in terms of what it reveals about how the first Christians worshiped. We know that the following things happened:

- They sang.
- They prayed.
- They laid hands on the sick, and trusted God for supernatural transformation of human lives before their very eyes.
- They ate together, remembering Jesus' last meal.
- They studied the Scriptures.
- The apostles and others shared first-hand experiences of their encounters with Christ and the changes that God had worked in their lives.

It is unclear whether they regularly collected an offering in a worship setting. It is unclear if they recited the Lord's Prayer. It is unclear what role, if any, primitive creeds played in their worship. It is unclear what Jewish worship traditions were retained. It is very clear that there was little if any distinction in dress or status between believers, with the exception that apostles were treated with a certain reverence, much as we would treat the New Testament record with reverence. This was due to the apostles' first-hand knowledge of Jesus.

It is also very clear that most of the regulations and practices that today's churches have about the above activities are not rooted in the New Testament, but in accumulated habit. As habits can be good or bad, we need to be able to assess our worship habits. Habits vary widely from church to church. What a Baptist church in South Carolina might consider "traditional worship," might be decidedly nontraditional in the context of, say, a Methodist church in west Africa. For this reason, I try to be careful with the term *traditional* when describing a worship service. For similar reasons, I try to avoid the word *contemporary* altogether, when talking about worship.

How do I assess a worship service? Very simply. I ask, "Is God being honored in the lives of these people?" And "Are these people truly connecting with God?" Sometimes it is hard to answer such questions as a guest observing for an hour and not getting to know the people. One of our worship team members reminded me once that a fifteen-year-old boy slumped over in a chair, not singing, looking terribly bored, may, in fact, be deeply captured by God's spirit and dealing inwardly with huge life choices that will largely determine the course of his life. Is that kid worshiping? Yes, if he is dealing with God in that moment, you'd better believe he is worshiping.

Reinventing an Existing Worship Service

There is more than one way to create a new worship community. A very good way is to create a growing network of small groups who come together to form that community. Another way is to open up a new worship hour or worship space at an existing location where worship already happens. Still another way is to gather a core of interested people, blitz the community with publicity, and give birth to a large worship community in one week. Still another way is to take an existing worship service and reinvent it. Each of these methods has its challenges and benefits. Our church has tried all of the above as we have started various new services across the years.

Our church grew for many years primarily through the magnetism of its worship experiences: down-to-earth preaching and heart-felt music. When we went through a disruptive music ministry leadership transition in the mid-'90s, worship attendance dipped briefly by about 200 per Sunday. The reason that attendance bounced back a few months later was because we changed the format of our middle (9:30 A.M.) worship service.

In 1994, Herb Sadler found himself at lunch with Lyle Schaller. Lyle asked Herb to tell him about our church. Herb mentioned that we had three Sunday morning services. When Lyle discovered that all three services were identical in format, he asked simply, "Why?" He could not understand why we would fish with the same bait three times in a row.

In the fall of '94, we altered the format of the 11 A.M. service slightly, removing the Apostle's Creed and the pulpit robes, replacing the opening hymn with a medley of choruses. The response of the people was mixed. We probably offended as many as we delighted (which is a normal consequence of tinkering with existing worship services). Once we lost our music leader a year later, we "circled the wagons," shifting back to one format, a spirited traditional service such as we had done for years, which we would try to do as well as we could three times in a row each Sunday.

In the spring of '96, I traveled to Ginghamsburg Church near Dayton, Ohio, to learn first-hand how they were pioneering new worship forms. As I examined the way this rapidly growing church worshiped in 1996, I identified the following keys:

1. The service was seamless. The whole thing was woven around a theme, with quick and intentional transitions between various elements. There was not simply an odd assortment of elements. There was a larger plot, a larger script which tied the message, drama, and music into a whole.
2. Almost all of the music had been written in the previous five years.
3. They used drama more to raise questions rather than to answer questions. The scripts enabled the pastor to respond to the issues raised. In this way, they avoided the preachy, corny tone that I had found common in worship drama up until then.
4. A large screen enabled video and still images to be projected throughout the service, images which supported and enhanced whatever else was happening.

I returned from Ohio deeply impressed by the pioneering work of Ginghamsburg Church. I also returned convinced that our church could incorporate three of these four characteristics into our worship. (It took several years before we would figure out how to do video projection in our sanctuary without destroying the aesthetics of the room. Had we known a couple years earlier there was a multimedia reformation about to sweep the church, it may have changed entirely the way we designed our enlarged sanctuary.)

Our worship leadership team decided we would seek to change the format of one of our existing services without providing advance warning. (Advance warning just makes people defensive.) We would make the changes incrementally during the summer, when people would be more apt to write off the new approach to summer informality. In the event that people did not respond positively, we would have no verbal commitment to the new direction, leaving a way to back-peddle if needed. This, in my opinion, is the only way to change the format of an existing service. We looked at our three services and decided that we would reinvent our 9:30 worship service slowly over the latter half of 1996.

We dropped the pulpit robes in June, as we had done each year in the Florida summer. The 9:30 service choir got a summer vacation. We put a praise ensemble up front to lead with contemporary Christian music. The music was very "Peter, Paul, and Mary" sounding at first, but it evolved over time. Eventually, drums were added, and the volume began to creep up. The quality of the music was excellent from day one, an absolute necessity when introducing a new style of music to a congregation.

I began writing five-minute dramas around the theme of the morning's message. I said if Kim Miller (who was the worship director at Ginghamsburg) can write a drama on Wednesday, cast it on Thursday, rehearse it on Friday and perform it on Saturday, WE CAN TOO. And we did. Later, Crosspoints and others began to produce decent scripts, but in 1996, most of the published scripts I found were generally more off-the-wall than we were ready for in our church. So I wrote most of our scripts. At first, I wrote, cast, and directed each drama to assure quality. Potential cast members were everywhere. I just had to ask. In late 1997, I began farming out the scripts to directors in the church, who then cast and produced the dramas with little input or oversight. In 1998, we began weaving in dramas by other writers, or purchasing scripts and changing the endings or adding characters to meet our needs.

The message at 9:30 remained the same as the other two services on most Sundays. Herb's down-to-earth approach did not need to be modified to fit the new format. In addition, our minister of music was able to make the shift from leading a traditional choir to also leading a praise ensemble. The abilities of our key worship leaders to function comfortably and effectively in the new environment were critical to the success of the "new" 9:30 service.

In the twelve months after we began these changes, the crowd at 9:30 grew from around 350 in average attendance to about 550. It would have grown even beyond that had we not been so critically short of parking places. The 9:30 service became the major port of entry into our church, with about half of the new people joining by profession of their faith in Christ. By making these changes, we were able to give a meaningful weekly worship experience to those in our community whom we were not before reaching.

Of course, there were a few detractors, who did not want to give away their worship service to the community. Some did not like the new music. Others detested the idea of drama in worship. Many of these people shifted to other services. Others eventually learned to like the new format, or at least, to tolerate it. We were clear throughout the months of transition that the 8:15 and 11:00 A.M. services would remain unchanged (meaning, in our context, that there would be organ-led hymns, the worship leaders would wear special clothing, and there would be a familiar order to things). Most church leaders will not get away with changing an existing service unless there are good, and relatively convenient, worship options, designed for those who are unhappy with the changes.

A Fast Start in a New Location

There are two questions I am asked regarding Gulf Breeze Church more often than any others. One is the question of how one church can operate effectively on two campuses. The other is how we got nearly 600 people to the first worship service at the East Campus and managed to hold on to a sizable crowd. Churches sometimes work for twenty years to accomplish such a thing. In 1999, it may have seemed to those looking on that we simply added water and stirred, producing in one week what would, by certain measures, be one of the strongest congregations in our area.

Three years after we reinvented the 9:30 service at the Main Campus, we launched our church's fourth Sunday morning service—a brand new worship community based at the Community Life Center, occurring simultaneously with the service mentioned above. Because this new worship service at this new location was a project fully sponsored and underwritten by an existing congregation, we were able to marshal significant financial and people resources. These resources would have taken years to gather had we started simply with a preacher appointed by the bishop to a piece of land in South Santa Rosa County. For this reason, I believe that what we did at the Community Life Center offers an extremely promising model for church extension.

When we began to plan for this fourth Sunday morning service, I returned to Ginghamsburg with a couple of others: the leader of our Main Campus sound team and a film producer from Pensacola. We attended the Ginghamsburg Media Reformation conference. Our primary mission was to think through the facility design considerations at the proposed Community Life Center in order to accommodate video projection (and production) as a part of our ministry. Later, we sent our new worship pastor back to Ginghamsburg to sit down face to face with Kim Miller and talk through logistics of weekly production and planning in order to lead such a worship service as we were planning. There is no doubt in my mind that without the pioneering work of the Ginghamsburg Church, we could not have done what we did as fast as we did it. A bouquet of thanks is due them from many churches across this land!

We decided that our East Campus service would be different from the Main Campus 9:30 service in the following ways:

1. The music would be edgier, with more of a concert feel.
2. There would be more casual dress among worship leaders.
3. Worshipers would have a choice of sitting in rows or around tables.
4. There would be coffee and food in the worship area.
5. Lighting would be more versatile, changing the desired ambiance at different parts of the worship service.
6. With a rear-projection system and a large video screen, the new service would incorporate visual graphics and film clips.
7. There would be no pulpit. The teaching pastor would simply stand before the congregation.

In order to start the new service effectively, we realized we would need an average attendance of at least 250 from the outset. This was based on the size of the room, which we knew would easily accommodate 750. We figured that to feel successful we needed the room to be at least one-third full. It is important that a room be perceived as "comfortably full." It was important, therefore, to gather a core group from the Main Campus who would commit to attending the new service for a period of time long enough to ensure that the service would take root. It was also important to generate hundreds of visitors in the first few weeks. The key to averaging 250, we believed, would be gathering 500 on the first Sunday, offering a quality experience, and responding appropriately to guests. I was not sure whether we could get 500. I would have been satisfied with 400 the first day.

To gather the core from the other three services, we did the following things:

1. In January 1999, some eight months prior to the first service, we included East Campus ministry opportunities in the mix for our members as they made their volunteering commitments for service in the coming year. A couple dozen persons volunteered for East Campus Sunday morning ministries, forming the beginnings of a leadership team.
2. In May, four months prior to the start of the service, we held a Sunday brunch after both the 9:30 and the 11:00 A.M. services in the Fellowship Hall at Main Campus. We called it an East Campus Brunch. We invited all worshipers verbally and in printed general announcements. In addition, we personally invited any people who had indicated an interest in helping start the new service. Approximately 200 attended the brunches. We gave a PowerPoint presentation about the many ministries anticipated at the East Campus. We then answered questions, many of which concerned the nature and time of the new worship service.
3. In June, our new East Campus worship pastor played his sax during a worship service at Main Campus. This was the first time that many people realized that the East Campus service would be of a quality comparable to what they had known at Main Campus. In each service following the sax piece, we shared the vision for the new service, inviting potential musicians and multimedia techies to get on board with the new service.
4. In July, the new East Campus worship leader led the worship band at the 9:30 Main Campus service for two weeks, further establishing his musical credibility.
5. On Sunday, August 15, five weeks prior to the first service, we kicked off our in-house publicity campaign for the new service. On this day and on the following Sunday, we placed cards in each of the worship bul-

letins on which people could commit to attend the new worship service for a period of three months. We realized that most people would either love the new service or hate it—if they loved it, they might stay for years; if they hated it, they would be gone in a few weeks, regardless of their length of commitment. Since more people would be willing to commit to a shorter time frame, we did not ask a six month or year long commitment from our pioneers. Over the next few weeks, approximately 150 people committed to the service, including band members and other leadership.

6. On Sunday, August 29, three weeks prior to the first service, we showed our first GBUMC-produced video, *Are You Having Fun Yet?*, in all three services. The video was narrated by me and our community recreation director. The new worship service was highlighted in the video along with the new recreation ministries. The last three minutes of the video featured a slide show of pictures following the construction of the building from ground breaking to completion over audio of Christian singer Billy Crockett singing "Would You Go There?"

7. On two different Sundays in the month prior to the grand opening, I preached all three services at Main Campus. Since the pastor they were used to hearing each week would not be the main preacher at the new service, it was important that everyone see and hear the person who would be leading the new service. A decision to attend this new service was not simply a decision to try a different service, but a decision that involved changing both the location of one's Sunday worship and one's preacher.

8. On Sunday, September 12, fifty of us gathered in a circle in the Community Life Center lobby at 8:00 A.M., marking the beginning of the East Campus Sunday morning ministries. We were a combination of band members, greeters, and tour guides for Grand Opening Sunday. Around 1,400 people came through the doors that morning. The tour ended in the gym, where people enjoyed brunch while the new Community Life Center Praise

Band sang, the audio-visual system was showcased, and I gave a brief welcome, with a commercial for the new service that started the next week. This was the first time the band had ever performed in public. Fortunately, they were very good. We had originally planned to have a sample service. Along the way, we shifted our energy to Grand Opening Sunday morning, since this would give us exposure to three or four times as many people as would come to a sample service. Our grand opening served the function of our sample service. I cannot imagine starting a new service without offering at least one sample service.

In each of the experiences above, a few more people decided to give the new service a try. We succeeded in communicating that the quality of the new worship service would be equal in every way to the quality of the Main Campus worship experiences. Since the perceived quality of our Main Campus worship services was very high, we could not have succeeded in the new service without demonstrating that its music and messages would be of comparable quality.

Of the 590 people who showed up for the first service on September 19, 1999, half were GBUMC members and half were community people. Of the 300 church people, many were present simply as a one-time gesture of support. And yet, the positive experience week after week brought still others.

The external public relations plan related to the launching of the Community Life Center is detailed in chapter five. We managed to attract an additional 300 persons from the community, most of whom had no active church affiliation. Our highway message board, the facility traffic from recreational programming, and word of mouth all worked together to keep a steady stream of first-time attenders throughout the fall.

Attendance at our new service drifted downward during the first few weeks, just as we had anticipated. Conventional wisdom suggests that the leaders of a new service, if that service starts with a bang on its first Sunday, can expect to see attendance cook down to about fifty percent of the level achieved on start-up Sunday. About three to six months along the way, the service should begin to grow. In our case, we bottomed out at the three month point, averaging in December 1999 about fifty-six percent of what we had to begin with on September 19. In the new year, it began to creep upward slowly, eclipsing 700 on Easter, but not consistently breaking above 400 until the summer of 2000, when we experienced our first noticeable, lasting attendance boost. By the time the service was two years old, we were regularly surpassing 500. A second East Campus service is set to begin in January 2002.

One of the major surprises of our East Campus worship community was the age diversity of the crowd, spread from infants to seventy-somethings. In January of 2000, about half the people in this service were baby boomers. We expected that. But there were also roughly equal numbers of adults older and younger than the baby boomers. Over the course of the first year, the Generation X group overtook the seniors in number, but the service kept its inter-generational feel.

This surprised us, as we had expected a younger crowd than we had at Main Campus. We had not expected a significant number of senior adults. We did not figure that seniors would respond to the style of the music, or to the extremely playful style of the service (which some might call irreverent). However, many seniors are not attracted to traditional services for a variety of reasons. Many of these people were unchurched young adults in the 1960s, and have been playing golf and tennis on Sundays for the last several decades. Others gave church a try along the way and had bad experiences that caused them to drop out.

In our first year as people joined the church, the East Campus crowd moved from being thirty-seven percent church members to about fifty percent members. The number of people from the Main Campus attending at the East Campus decreased.

The balance of seekers, new believers, and long-time church attenders has been very constructive for all parties involved. We are convinced that seekers and believers can experience God in the same room so long as leaders are committed to speaking and to making music in a language and style that is accessible and meaningful to the wider community.

Perhaps the biggest surprise has been the number of long-time church people who have come to share in the vision of what this service accomplishes. One after another, they talk about how they expected to hate the service, but have come to love it. For some of these people, who move back and forth between services of varying styles, they love the comfort of traditional rituals, but they now also love experiencing God in fresh new ways.

It Takes a Team

In the summer of 1999, even before Jeremy Morse, our worship/music pastor, moved to town, he began mailing me tapes of various kinds of Christian music in current circulation, with evaluation forms for my feedback on each song. He and I found a consensus in terms of the range and style of music that we thought were appropriate for what we were trying to do. We found a place to start musically, with the agreement that we would adapt and change as experience warranted. We chose music with an edge to it, music with strong guitar, percussion, and keyboard. We chose to go with our instincts on the music at first, rather than poll a wide group. We realized that there was no way to accommodate everyone's vision in a new worship service. The easier and less divisive approach was to make a call, and evaluate it in light of the response during the first weeks of the service.

The guiding consideration in the choice of musical style was that it would be an accessible style of music for non-church persons and young adults in our community—the two groups who have the greatest difficulty feeling at home at church. In other words, we thought of the community's needs before the church's needs.

Jeremy arrived in Gulf Breeze three months prior to the first service. Upon arrival, he was faced immediately with major purchasing decisions on musical and technical equipment. Then he began to gather the musicians into a band and the techies into a multi-media team.

In August, we convened a design team for our new service. We held a Saturday retreat in the Studio, still bare of furnishings. The design team consisted of the following people: the music/worship pastor, the teaching pastor (me), two band members, the drama coordinator, our youth pastor, our multimedia director, and a long-time church member from Main Campus (who was a die-hard Lenny Kravitz fan). In the early days of the service design, the church's senior pastor was also an occasional presence in team meetings. The median age of our design team was in the mid-30s, reflecting what we thought would be the mix of the new service, a blend of baby boomers and Generation X. The group was hand-picked, with great care given to the synergy created. They were a blend of paid and unpaid leaders. There were a couple of movie buffs who could always rattle off titles and scenes of movies which illustrated various points and ideas.

We agreed that this design team would convene each Tuesday morning for two hours at the Main Campus (a central location for all) to evaluate the previous week's service, wrestle with the text and theme of the upcoming service, and brainstorm ways of building community and advancing the theme. The team met for nine months, taking a break in the summer of 2000. In the fall of 2000, we adopted a simpler worship planning process with a smaller team.

The larger circle of input had been helpful, however, in creating and evaluating the service during its first year.

Regardless of the changing planning styles and production schedules, the following things have remained constant in our preparation for worship each week:

- *The worship team works on a week by week basis,* as a rule. The teaching pastor may have themes planned for a couple months or more, however. Where we see complex videos on the horizon, we give the video production people a bit more lead time. (It is amazing, however, how often quality video productions can be produced in about 72 hours time from conception to completion.)
- *Each worship service is driven by a theme and a life need,* brought to the table by the teaching pastor, or the person bringing the message that particular week.
- *The team works to advance the week's theme* by suggesting possible video clips, pieces of music, visual props, graphic images, etc.
- *Production of various service elements is assigned to respective people.*
- *Dialogue is ongoing* through the week between the teaching pastor and worship pastor, with ideas emerging and changing throughout the week.
- *There is often a second meeting late in the week* to tie the service together and create an order of events; a script of sorts.

Community-Building

One of the down sides to starting a service with a crowd, rather than with a small group, is that you begin on day one with a blob—an assortment of people without relationships and without a sense of common purpose—a group of strangers. It is both our goal for the long-term and, to a lesser extent, our goal in each service, to move this blob from the level of strangers to friends, from crowd to community, from individuals to church. One of the ways we do this is with a five-minute experience that happens toward the beginning of each service that we call community time. The goals of community time are to welcome people; to put them at ease, to break the ice, to laugh together, and often to learn about something that is happening in the community or to get to know one of our leaders better. There are weeks when community time is directly setting up and advancing the service theme. Other weeks, it is more low-key. It may range from a simple pastoral greeting to a full-blown quiz show where we go into the congregation and ask for volunteers to answer trivia questions about the staff.

Community time is not the announcement hour. We occasionally use community time as a forum to promote *one* specific ministry event or opportunity, but usually with live interview or specially produced video. It is not the time for multiple announcements. Announcements are better offered in print, so that all the information we need to know is placed in our hands and can travel home with us. A laundry list of announcements on the front end of a worship service is deadening. Most people will be turned off, literally. They will be left in a daze, minds wandering in a hundred directions, zinging back and forth from this event to that. Spoken announcements in worship do not invite us into the event at hand.

One week, the theme of the service was *Leaving Home*, and we used the Dr. Seuss book, *Oh the Places You'll Go*, in terms of visual graphics throughout the service. During community time that day we played Dr. Seuss trivia and gave away various Dr. Seuss books. Another week, the theme was *Patience*. We started the service with a drama of waiting in a grocery store check-out line, which began by my selecting volunteers from the congregation to play cameo roles. Different churches will find different atmospheres that will work in drawing people out of themselves into what is happening around them. Some churches are intentionally very serious in the way they start a service. Obviously we are more subdued in the way we would start a Good Friday service than in how we would start a service at Christmas. In every case, I simply want to see people who are not used to being at church take down their barriers and defenses at the front end of the service. If you think about the movies or the worship services where you had tears toward the end, you might be amazed how many times you laughed toward the beginning. Laughter opens us up to feel deeply. Powerful, evocative, Christ-centered music will be felt more deeply on the heels of laughter, and will open us up not only to feel deeply, but to be changed as we move to experience the truth and challenge of the good news . . .

Order and Flow

. . . which brings us to order and flow. For centuries, the order and flow of Christian worship was defined by the movements of the Catholic Mass. In most Protestant traditions, we can mark traditions of order and flow in worship that, while not spanning multiple centuries, span multiple decades. For the average long-time church-goer, these traditions might as well span millennia, because they reach back before our own personal remembrances. If there is a definition of *traditional* in this terribly pluralistic age, it would be "anything that was around before we were."

In most established churches seeking to make their worship more accessible to persons outside their traditions, it will be necessary to retain at least one worship service which is perceived by the long-timers as traditional, even as they attempt to create services that are not limited by the constraints of tradition. Many long-time members will be supportive of new initiatives in worship and ministry, in prayer, in giving, even in volunteering, so long as we do not take away from them the form of worship which has strengthened, inspired, and comforted them through the years. The Community Life Center's building was built largely by the gifts of persons who would never dream of worshiping there on a regular basis. Had our church leaders not had the wisdom to understand worship style as a "both/and" issue rather than an "either/or" issue, we might not have been able to marshal the resources and efforts of such a broad coalition to advance a bold and significant ministry like the Community Life Center.

My mother lives in another state. But were she a resident of Gulf Breeze, Florida, and a member of our church, she would attend the 11:00 worship hour at Main Campus. My mother has attended church for many decades. She likes a predictable order to worship, week to week. She also is typical of millions of mainline church members all across America, who wants to see her church reach new people for Christ. Given an opportunity to do so, she will give generously, work long hours, and pray hard for new ministry initiatives. My mother led me to Christ. I know her heart, and I have seen that heart mirrored in many long-time members in every place I have served. But it would be difficult to effectively lead my mother in a worship service that also engaged a significant number of unchurched persons.

It is extremely unconstructive on the part of traditionalists to demonize those of us who are seeking to share a very old faith with a new culture. It is equally unconstructive on the part of progressives to demonize those traditionalists who just can't find God amid drums and pounding rock music.

There is no set order for the kind of service we do at our East Campus, except that I have learned that it is best not to offer the message until several songs have been sung. We sometimes vary the plot, depending in part on what we are trying to communicate in the service. We don't even print a road map of where the service is going in the bulletin. People are left guessing at times what is going to happen next. But that is not unlike a good movie. Increasing numbers of people prefer surprise to predictability. People who have no deep affection for traditional orders of worship seem to really enjoy twists in the plot. A major factor in the energy and expectancy that people bring to East Campus worship is that they come wondering "what are they gonna do this week?"

The only word of warning to any worship leadership team who wants to shift elements around from week to week: if you are going to move the time when the offering is collected and you do not provide ample notice that the plates are about to be passed, you will reduce the amount of money that gets into the plate. Whether the offering happens early in the service or late, we always tell everyone what is about to happen at that point.

Kids in Worship

It is absolutely imperative that age-appropriate experiences for children under the age of twelve be provided simultaneously with worship experiences designed primarily for adults. Long-time church attenders sometimes protest that this keeps the church from training children to worship. I always respond that millions of children and youth who were bored to tears on church pews in the '60s and '70s have abandoned organized religion altogether. Teaching children that church is boring is not my idea of good faith development. And sometimes even the most engaging of worship experiences can be really boring for a child.

So a church should offer Sunday school and/or children's worship at the same times that the main worship services are offered. At the very least, there should be a children's ministry available during the hour of the service that attracts the largest number of community guests. Almost invariably, this will be the least traditional worship service. However, if a church also has a vision for growing its more traditional services, children's activities need to be offered simultaneously with those services as well.

Children's sermons in the main worship service are fun for most adults, and not fun for most children anymore. A few times each year, we take our East Campus worship outdoors onto our lawn. When we do this, we design a service in which elementary kids can participate, sometimes including a children's sermon, in which one of us relates the theme of the service to kids, with adults observing. Ninety percent of the children's sermons I have seen in my life are either too abstract for a child's understanding or too loosely connected to scriptural truth. The punch lines are designed for adults. We would serve our children better to free them from this silly weekly ritual and look instead for ways to make the worship hour the most exciting hour of the week for our children.

We allow families the choice of bringing their children into worship or taking them to Sunday school/children's worship. Different kids need different things. Because of the music and audio visuals, many older elementary children enjoy the main service. However, many adults who are new to the faith, enjoy being able to explore their relationship with Christ for an hour without having to wrestle with their wiggly six-year-old.

The children's areas in the building should, of course, be the among the best looking areas in the whole facility. Bright, recently renovated (last five years) space with teachers present at least fifteen minutes before starting time tells parents that a church offers quality children's ministry.

Sharing the Good News

I really expected the task of preaching to get harder when we began the East Campus service. For seventeen years, I had developed sermons in solo mode. I figured that the involvement of a team effort would muddy the waters and lengthen the process. I worried that integrating graphics and video would make it harder still.

It did not get harder. It got slightly easier. This has been a happy surprise. I have a hunch that a similar happy surprise is in store for a lot of pastors in this decade. My weekly prep time for a Sunday message is about the same now as when I was preaching in a more traditional setting. It takes a few weeks to adjust to the new process of sermon development so that one thinks visually as well as orally. But I am told by all parties that the quality of my preaching is consistently better.

One of the best decisions we made in the new worship setting was to have no pulpit. I just sit on a $10 wooden barstool from Wal-Mart. Occasionally I stand to make a point or to interact with the video screen. I place key notes in my Bible, such as teaching points, key words, and transitions, which the team in back are expecting in order to run the visuals on the screen behind me in sync with the message.

I sometimes forget to say certain things. Occasionally, I get lost. However, what I gain in terms of my connection with the congregation without a pulpit and manuscript far outweighs any verbal meanderings that might occur. Notes and pulpits are barriers. Barriers to eye contact. Barriers to physical visibility. Barriers to a sense of dialogue and authenticity. Remove those barriers from all the preachers in America this week, and the quality of preaching in many churches would rise to the level of that experienced in the book of Acts. Those were rather ordinary folks who preached in the book of Acts. Add the help of audio-visuals, and most preachers today are capable of even more effective communication than was possible in the first century.

The availability of visual images and film clips means that the preacher is less pressed to paint pictures in words. Illustrations become less complex. Simple life experiences supported by photos are now as effective as the most poignant stories I used to paint with words alone. The right film clip every two or three weeks is more effective still. The key to using film clips is the first sentence out of the pastor's mouth after the film clip, words that nail the point of the illustration so that people will remember it a week later. People ask me how long I preach. I really don't know anymore. Our service stays in the range of an hour, or maybe sixty-five minutes. The message may be interrupted by an interview or a video presentation. It may flow out of a drama. It may be broken up into pieces that happen over the course of the service. We view worship as a whole, not as a bunch of disconnected parts. The length of the entire service is more important than the length of any particular element, so long as the service does not feel "bogged down" at any point. The actual amount of time that I am up and talking can vary from fifteen to thirty-five minutes, depending on the service.

Inviting Response

There are several good models available in terms of inviting and receiving acts of commitment from people in worship. The only rule I can find here is that we should always provide clear instructions to people as to how they can respond to the good news that has been proclaimed. For some churches, this will mean an altar call. In the first year of the East Campus service, I gave only one altar call, and (to my surprise) more than a hundred people came forward that day. All the other Sundays ended without an altar call. More recently, we have instituted an altar prayer time at the end of most services. We also put communication cards in everyone's hands so they can indicate if they would like a call or would like to join the church.

Various people follow up on these requests weekly. We make it clear that you do not have to stand up in front of the church and be introduced in order to join Gulf Breeze Church. Interestingly, the day we clarified this issue a few years ago, the number of new members jumped. To this day, I have never been able to detect any difference in the quality of commitment demonstrated by those who agree to be introduced in worship and those who are a bit more bashful.

Usually the primary invitation to commitment is not related to joining the church. We are finding that fewer and fewer people are motivated by the idea of belonging to the church as an institution. So we talk less about membership and more about various aspects of Christian commitment, ranging from giving to serving to praying.

A word of warning: a worship community cannot, in and of itself, make disciples of people. That process requires more one-on-one attention than is possible in a worship service. But worship always should offer an invitation to discipleship. Worship can and should offer gateways for people towards the kinds of activities that will cause them to grow spiritually. It is wise to start a network of small relational groups six to twelve months prior to the launch of a new worship service, with additional group leaders trained and ready to start new groups as masses of people respond to Christ in the new service. Such groups can enable young believers to grow into full-fledged disciples of Jesus Christ. We failed to prepare small group leaders prior to the launch of the first East Campus service. Thus, we did not have an adequate discipling system ready to take the people God sent us beyond the worship hour. We have been playing catch up from the first Sunday, constantly looking for fresh ways and for opportunities to invite those gathered for Sunday morning worship to experience a more intimate community, where permanent life transformation is more likely to be achieved.

CHAPTER SEVEN

Birthing Pains

There Is an Easier Way

In local church ministry, doing nothing is usually easier than doing something, and often more popular. It is sure easier to circle the wagons and get comfortable than to take risks and push ourselves to change in order to widen our circle. At any point along the journey, a church can reach a point of contentedness and decide to coast. A church does not have to keep adding services. A church does not have to go to a second campus. In fact, most churches in the late '90s that were in the same position as my church would have concluded that they were big enough. They would have chosen to concentrate their energy on enhancing the quality of current ministries and simply creating greater spiritual depth among the membership. Our population growth areas were, by then, many miles from where our church was located. We had enough youth and children to fill a room, a bus, or a whole building anytime we wanted. The same monies that we raised to build our second campus could have renovated our church offices, built us a pipe organ, and provided us a plush and elegant fellowship hall.

If the crowd eventually became uncomfortably light at one of our three worship services, we could have consolidated to two services, resulting in a perception of greater success. With more people at the remaining two services, the perceived quality of the worship experience for our people would have risen to new heights (at least for those who didn't quit when their service was discontinued). With fewer new people constantly streaming in, the people already present could have gotten to know each other better, enhancing the sense that Gulf Breeze Church was truly their spiritual family. Parking congestion would have eased. People could have claimed their "regular seat," without strangers getting in the way.

Almost everyone who was a part of our church could have been lulled into blissful contentedness, without all the changes we introduced! We could have all left church each Sunday feeling personally uplifted and deeply satisfied about the strength and success of our ministry.

Just think what the pastors might have accomplished without all the hours gobbled up by expansion efforts. They would have been freer to serve on denominational committees and the boards of local charities. Our senior pastor could have run for bishop, further adding to the prestige and successful image of our church.

But time after time, the leaders of our church chose the harder path. Not the path of least resistance, but the uphill path. Each time we did this, we "spent a bullet" and strained our church's internal consensus. Each time we changed and pushed in order to reach out, we alienated and confused loyal members who were perfectly happy with the way things were. At every turn, there have been birthing pains.

Bill Hinson, pastor of First United Methodist Church in Houston, a congregation that served as an early pioneer in a multi-campus ministry, shared with us a lunch conversation between himself and Charles Allen, the legendary pastor who preceded him at First Church, Houston. In that conversation, from atop a nearby skyscraper, looking down upon the historic downtown campus of First United Methodist, Allen essentially said to Hinson, "Just preach to these people and love them and they will be very happy." Hinson, however, saw an increasingly difficult future for his church with a downtown-only base of ministry. He led his church to take the harder path, alienating quite a few folks in the process. But in taking the harder path, he assured that First

United Methodist Church would remain a spiritual leader in Houston well into the twenty-first century.

We Need to Keep Pushing Even When Some Folks Do Not Understand

Gently, gracefully, steadily, we keep pushing. In *Generation to Generation,* Edwin Freidman talks about the differentiated leader who is more concerned with leading in the right direction than in keeping everybody happy on the journey. Occasionally this leader looks over her shoulder to see if the people are still following. Occasionally, this backward glance reveals that the leader has lost most of the flock, so the leader circles back to gather all he can. But this non-anxious, differentiated leader is most concerned with moving in the right direction, allowing the people the freedom to come along or to stay back.

My church has kept pushing itself out of its comfort zone because we have believed that the proactive hospitality of God compelled us to do so. We have pushed so hard because God never showed us a stopping place. Through the years, we have discovered that our church's good health results from being an open, growing system. We have enjoyed the gifts and contributions of new people. We have enjoyed freedom from the development of a controlling elite, who can grow ever more powerful in churches where there is little turnover in membership. Eventually, in our case, continued growth became a treasured part of our church's culture. After more than twenty years of consecutive increases in average worship attendance, we realized that to cease reaching out would be the most radical change possible for our church. Having flung open our doors, we realized that we could never close them without doing damage to our church's very nature.

There were several individuals who were initially opposed to our East Campus project. In most cases, these were persons who were outside the decision-making loop in the early stages of the project. Rumors abounded. Some feared that this was the first step toward relocation (even though the new site was clearly too small for a full reloca-tion). Others feared that the church was going to split. Many feared that the project would fail, since it was eight miles from the Main Campus. Others feared that the Main Campus would begin to fail, in the shadow of a fast-growing, high-energy East Campus. All we knew to do was to sit down and listen to people talk about their fears and reas-sure them in all honesty that we were praying and planning with the hope and intent that none of these fears would materialize.

After the East Campus had been open for a year, almost every concerned individual was greatly relieved. Most who had been skeptical were growing more comfortable with the two-campus concept. They saw the tremendous success of the Community Life Center, the overall growth of the church, and the fact that so little changed at the Main Campus. The leaders at First Methodist in Houston noted the very same phenomenon in the months after they opened their West Campus. Once a slightly unconventional venture succeeds, everyone wants on the bandwagon.

Had we not listened to the concerns of the detractors, several families certainly would have left the church. It is common for a few folks to leave whenever churches make major decisions. Had a couple dozen people left, the church would have survived and still enjoyed a burst of growth with the addition of the East Campus. But I am so glad that we took the time to listen to people and to reassure them. It was a tedious and exhausting task. But as a result of that pastoral care, not one family left the church over the deci-sion to expand to a second campus. The pastoral listening was not anxious listening, it was not public opinion polling to see which way the church should go. We listened simply for the purpose of saying to those who disagreed, "We love you."

Had we not entered the project with a long-tenured pastoral leader, it would have been more difficult to hold the church together through such a major shift in paradigms. The much less radical decision by our church fifteen years earlier simply to build a new sanctuary next door to the old one generated considerably more vehement opposition, and a few people did leave at that time. In that case, there were still a number of people in the church who had not bought into the open door community church vision.

In no case should a church feel constrained to wait for one hundred percent consensus among its people. To wait for one hundred percent consensus often will only serve to empower a few controlling, negative personalities who wish to derail change.

A Shrinking Core of Decision Makers

The administrative leadership, which I would define as those teams of people who oversee staffing issues, financial issues, and facility issues, involves an ever-shrinking percentage of the members of most vital churches. Most growing churches will discover significantly fewer people on administrative committees with 2,000 members than they had with 1,000. In churches of all sizes, there is a definite trend away from committee and toward ministry team.

As we pushed and changed, a steady stream of fresh leadership kept entering our ranks. Most of these people never found their way onto a committee. They simply caught a vision for ministry at some level and plugged in with a ministry team. At the same time, a few folks did find their way to the four central administrative committees of the church. We have sought to keep a continuity of leadership at the hub. So, while most people never found their way to a committee, a few honorable souls never found their way off. But in every case, these individuals were requested to remain in administrative leadership because (1) they shared the vision of the church as an ever-growing network of ministries offering hospitality, hope, and healing to all persons, and (2) they had gifts and perspectives which were needed at the leadership table. I will say again that we would rather see gifts used in front-line ministry than in administration. We have, thus, sought to tie up as few people as possible in administrative work.

We have continued four key administrative groups, which we call committees. In most churches, committees tend to be about procedure and decision. Teams tend to be about delivering ministry. Outside central administration, we do not have committees anymore. Everything is done by teams of people who come together around common purposes in ministry. Even our administrative committees function with a team spirit. These committees, consisting of a central leadership group, a finance group, a personnel group, and a board of trustees, often look and act more like teams than committees because they are comprised of persons with an unusual alignment of vision and an eye on ministry. They understand money, staff, and buildings simply to be means of ministry, not ends in themselves. Rarely do I see voting take place in any of our groups where close to one hundred percent consensus has not been realized prior to the vote. Fewer formal votes are necessary in such a climate. Most decisions are reached through prayerful listening to one another and to the Spirit. The work is divided among the members according to gifts. There is extraordinarily high trust among the members. And there is representation from the finance, personnel, and trustee groups on the central group. Many large churches are streamlining their administrative structure even beyond this level of complexity. More critical than how many people are serving in such leadership is the question of who is serving. Choosing the right people, people who buy into the vision, is essential. Often, in church turn around projects, until new leaders can be rotated into decision-making groups, and a few old ones can be rotated out, teamwork cannot begin.

When it comes to major new initiatives, such as a decision to purchase land and develop a second church campus, it is important that a consensus be built among the ranks of the administrative leadership as quickly as possible—which is very doable if these people all share a similar vision and set of values in terms of where the church is headed. However, since the leadership team is relatively small, it is also important that there be adequate time set aside for helping the rest of the church catch up and get on board with the vision and the recommendations. Some of the people outside the leadership team have been part of smaller churches in the past, where a high percentage of active members were involved in administrative leadership. They may be used to a democratic process where almost all of the major decisions (and even some not so major) are made by referendum at the grass roots level. The idea that plans are being formed quietly, and often behind the scenes, may be disconcerting to some of these people, especially if they do not understand or support the plans that are coming out of such behind-the-scenes deliberations.

Hindsight Is 20-20 . . . but If We Had It to Do over Again . . .

Every major mistake we made in our East Campus project had to do with money. To begin with, we could have raised more of it. And we should have done three things up front as a part of our first phase, rather than waiting until later. Because of concerns over budget, we (1) under-built parking, (2) underestimated the staff required, and (3) did not pay adequate attention to communication systems. If we had known how successful the venture was going to be, we could have addressed all of these issues from day one. In the future, I would go so far as to cut square footage if that was what it took to assure that money would be left on the table for staffing, communications, and adequate off-street parking to support the worship service capacity.

Raising Money

In terms of capital fund-raising, the most important issue in choosing a coach/consultant should not be *how much has this person helped other churches to raise,* but, rather, *how in sync is this person with the personality and vision of our church?* We chose an excellent capital stewardship coach, who had helped another church build a second campus. But our coach did not fit our church's unique culture. There is no telling how much greater the giving might have been had we found a coach who was really on our page in terms of theology, language, and culture. We pledged enough to entirely underwrite the East Campus first phase, and for this we thank God. But we would not have been pinched in key areas had we raised what we were capable of raising. We raised one and a half times our annual ministry budget in special pledges to be paid over thirty-six months. Churches who are well coached in the art of inviting special gifts often receive twice this in pledges. If we had it to do over again, we would look for a capital stewardship consultant who really understood our church.

Parking

In terms of parking, we originally built about half what we should have built. Our leadership simply did not anticipate that the new worship service would take root as fast as it did, with as many people as it did. We started with off-street parking for about 300 people. We added a gravel lot two months into the new service, a quick fix that required no county permitting. With the gravel lot, we increased our parking to accommodate about 450 people. It is no coincidence that the Sunday morning service grew in attendance until we approached 450, and then it plateaued. It was fourteen months after our grand opening before we secured county approval to add more permanent parking. An entire new site plan had to go before the various boards.

As of the end of 2000, our off-street parking accommodates about 550 people (based on the average number of people per car on Sunday mornings). This enabled attendance to grow beyond 500. We knew all along we would need this much parking eventually; in fact, our plans call for much more parking in the future, as we add other buildings to our East Campus. We were simply unsure of what unexpected expenses might jump out at us, so we held back on parking. In the end, costs skyrocketed and we paid considerably more for our parking than we would have if we had built it all in the beginning. We also adversely impacted our worship attendance for over a year, running off who knows how many people who could not find a parking space. It was an expensive mistake.

We weren't the first church ever to make such an error. Cutting back on parking is often seen as a way to stretch building dollars. Such cutbacks unintentionally undermine growth in participation of the ministries that will happen in our facilities. Whenever we undermine growth in worship attendance, we also undermine growth in a church's financial resources.

At 2.2 passengers per vehicle, our Sunday morning ministry on our East Campus is at the high end of vehicle capacity for churches across North America. Most churches now average less than two persons per vehicle, some as low as 1.5. It is common in many places for families of four to come in three cars. When one family member is teaching a class or serving in some capacity, the rest of the family comes separately. Where there are teenagers, it is common for still another car to appear. The number of persons per household is also falling in almost every community, meaning there will be fewer persons in each automobile. The fewer persons per vehicle, the more parking spaces that are needed to support a comparable attendance. No matter how big we make a building, if we fail to provide the necessary amount of parking to support the building's capacity, it will be extremely difficult to fill that building to eighty percent of its capacity on a regular basis.

Staffing

With staffing, our greatest errors came in the area of support staff. We needed two full-time building maintenance workers from day one. We budgeted for one. With a facility in use eighty hours a week, old formulas of staffing based solely on Sunday morning attendance went out the window!

We also needed a paid director of the welcome desk from day one. We planned only for volunteers at the welcome desk for the first year as a cost-saving measure. The new facility helped to create a burst of volunteer energy that we harnessed to fill about forty hours a week at the welcome desk. Most of the volunteers were simply outstanding in the care they showed to each inquiry from the public. We could not have made it without them. We still could not make it without them.

But too many shifts went unfilled. The phone sometimes would ring unanswered in the middle of the day or, even worse, go to voice mail. Occasionally, volunteers were not adequately briefed and trained so as to be able to relay information to the public. People would wander in off the street and ask questions like "What exactly is this place?" There was no consistency from hour to hour what answer they might hear.

Thousands of people accessed information via the welcome desk, either in person or on the phone, during our first year. In many cases, this would be the very first encounter people would ever have with Gulf Breeze United Methodist Church. If they encountered a trained volunteer, their first contact was probably extraordinary. I am sure, however, that many people's first impression of us was less than favorable. I fear that for hundreds of people, their first experience of the Community Life Center was calling to discover either no answer or to find someone who was not adequately equipped to serve them. Until the position could be filled, I simply gave up my administrative assistant for several hours each week. It was more important that someone competent be on the front lines than it was for me to have administrative help in my office.

Thankfully, the recreation ministry had such a positive cash flow in their first series of summer day camps, that the profit was able to begin the funding of a welcome desk coordinator starting with the fall of 2000. She has made ALL the difference in the world!

Communication Systems Between Campuses

Though we developed a fairly good communications network linking the two campuses, this network came together many months after the East Campus opened. We could have spent a gazillion dollars and brought in a company to fix this problem at the time we moved in. But in the case of phone and computer networking between remote sites, there are multiple solutions, changing monthly with the advance of technology, some of which are far less expensive than others. We finally discovered an economical way to connect the sites. We added voice mail to the system at the East Campus about a year after opening.

Because we did not start early enough on this, we ended up having to learn how to be one staff on two campuses without the aid of e-mail or voice mail. The East Campus staff felt, at times, like they were in a time warp—they would get snail mail memos from Main Campus a day late, or phone messages would be lost between shifts of volunteers. We waited for months for Internet access. Finally, the switchboard at Main Campus gained the ability to route callers directly to us at the East Campus. These technical inconveniences were minor compared to the way we had inconvenienced the public by not providing adequate staffing at our welcome desk.

It is no easy thing for a staff to shift to a two-site config-uration. The stress of learning how to work and communi-cate efficiently over a span of eight miles would have been much reduced had we solved our communications issues during the year before we opened the facility rather than during the year after it opened.

Certain Challenges Are Inevitable

Whether a church is expanding its ministry, starting a new ministry, or planting a new campus, there are some unavoidable challenges that can be expected. And the more ambitious a church is in its dreams, the more critical and troubling these thorny issues can become.

Small Group Development

Generally speaking, when churches (or new worship communities) begin as a movement of small groups, the small group side of community life is much easier to grow than when we seek to graft small groups onto a long-estab-lished church that has no prior commitment to this area.

Our East Campus service started as a crowd. The core constituency was adults born between 1945 and 1964—baby boomers. It is much easier to gather a quick crowd and get off to a fast start in worship with this age group than with young adults. It is also much harder to move people from mass worship to discipleship than vice versa.

Moving people from the East Campus service into small group experiences has been difficult. Two years into that service's life, we had about ninety adults a week in smaller group connections, up from fifty a year earlier. This repre-sented less than twenty-five percent of our adults on a typ-ical Sunday. A large percentage continues to be content with a one-hour commitment. The key to our success in devel-oping small groups will be the covenant among our leaders, beginning with staff, to be involved in such a group. Without that commitment at the core, we would likely continue to have less than one-third of our adults participating in such disciple-building groups and relationships.

Financial Uncertainty

No church ever knows how much money is going to come in, nor when it is going to come. For this reason, Gulf Breeze Church has, for several years, made financial decisions, based in large part upon the pledges of our people. We share the dreams, and we trust the people. They collectively tell us what they are willing and able to do financially. We factor in a little room for growth, but we are conservative. We challenge our people, collect pledges, establish a likely income scenario, and then budget to that scenario. We do not budget first and then dog our people to give to an arbitrary budget goal. Because we budget this way, we have a history of running surpluses rather than deficits. The surplus enables a bit of financial elbow room when growth demands more spending in a particular area or when unforeseen needs or opportunities suddenly arise. Accumulated surpluses enabled quick purchase of land within days of our decision to expand to two campuses. This is the up side of conservative financial planning.

The flip side is this. Churches that are very conservative in terms of estimated income tend to under-budget. Because we typically under-forecast our income, we sometimes wait too long to add needed staff positions or to make badly needed investments in facilities and equipment. We always seem to get where we need to be, but we are a bit slow at times. Each of the mistakes that I cited earlier in this chapter were, in part, based in our fiscal conservatism. There is no simple solution to this dilemma. There are dangers and benefits both in over-budgeting and under-budgeting. Every church just has to work this matter out before God.

Leader Gaps

It is amazing how faithful God is in raising up leaders. As I have watched the East Campus ministry teams move from one leader (myself) in early 1999 to scores of leaders, I have just marveled over and again at how people with the right gifts just seem to drop out of the sky. There is a time and a season for every ministry to explode. And usually that time is marked by the emergence of leadership.

Our recreation ministry offers a prime example of how a leader can make a difference. We had virtually no recreation ministry in 1997. At that time, it was all we could do to get one adult volleyball or basketball team together for the community church league. Our underdevelopment was in part related to our lack of recreational facilities, but was primarily due to the fact that we had not yet invested in strong leadership.

We made a decision to provide facilities and an excellent central leader for recreational ministries. That leader, Dan Pezet, then developed a hundred other leaders. They came out of the woodwork, rallying around a clear new commitment that our church had to recreation as a means toward our mission. In a twelve-month period, we went from having one of the poorest recreation ministries I have seen to having one of the best—all because of leadership. And once we found the right leader, other leaders began to emerge.

At every stage of a growing church's journey, there are the uncharted frontiers. In these frontiers, there are many things we would like to do, but it may not yet be the time to forge ahead. Churches need to be focused on first things first, building ministries one by one as God leads. Sometimes God will lead a church to find a leader who will develop other leaders in order to build a ministry area. Other times, God lifts up people with a passion for a certain task. They show up one day on the doorstep of the pastor's office with a dream and a willingness to go to work. In both types of situations, ministry explodes where often very little had happened before.

One of the most difficult aspects of leading a church is seeing the gaps, the things that need to be done, but which are not being done well, if at all. Usually, these gaps are painfully obvious to pastors. But until God reveals that "Now is the time," and provides the leadership, we have to live with the gaps, and often limp along as best we can. Every church lives with these gaps, and by God's grace, lives through them.

Acoustics

Okay, so the Mormons got lucky. Their engineers built a tabernacle with perfect acoustics. The chances of this happening to my church or yours, however, are about nil. So let's just accept that whenever we build space to assemble people, there will be serious acoustical challenges. I don't care how much you plan to spend on audio and accoustical engineers in the planning process; there will still be acoustical quirks in most worship spaces. And it is very hard to know exactly what the quirks will be until after construction is completed. I have come to believe that accoustical engineering is part voo-doo.

In each of the last two building projects at Gulf Breeze that included new worship space, there was about a year of acoustical chaos that followed. In each case, tens of thousands of dollars were spent over and above what was originally budgeted. In each case, money eventually solved the problems.

Whenever a church is building a new worship space, I recommend that they use experts in planning and purchasing the original equipment for that space and to set aside additional funds should they be necessary. I also recommend that the congregation be informed that it will take several months to iron out all the sound system issues, but that it will get better!

Our sound/acoustics low point at the Community Life Center came at the worst possible moment, during our first Christmas Eve service, with a packed house. We were still dealing with all original equipment and original equalization settings, set by a professional who did not quite understand what we were trying to accomplish in terms of sound in a non-traditional service. In addition, someone had turned on a separate set of building-wide, public-address speakers the day before the Christmas Eve service, resulting in a split second delay echo throughout the service. Many people left discouraged and depressed. I am sure some left intending never to return. I wish I could say that by sharing our experience, other churches could prevent such from happening, but I cannot. Acoustics are a challenge everywhere. All we can do is pray for patience and work as fast and as wisely as possible to fix the problems.

Acoustical wall panels and ceiling baffles can solve the acoustical issues in many rooms for a modest expense in comparison to the overall cost of construction. The wall panels alone did wonders for us! Building committees responsible for worship space construction, please note: until the acoustics are good, the building is still under construction.

Us and Them

Despite our best efforts to teach our people that we are one church on two campuses, some of them still don't get it. A few speak of "this church and that church." Others are distrustful of "those people" at the other campus. Because our worship is so different from service to service, some people think this difference separates the campuses. Thankfully, we have maintained a significant core of people who float back and forth between the Main Campus and the East Campus in worship. There are also hundreds of others who regularly attend events or classes at a campus other than the one at which they worship. These people work alongside the pastors in demonstrating a sense of ownership in both campuses. The "us and them" thing is a part of human nature, and is unavoidable. We cannot eliminate it, but we can minimize it. We have given many of our staff oversight of ministries on both campuses. We have rotated some East Campus-based staff to the Main Campus every few Sundays and Main Campus-based staff to the East Campus occasionally. We can hold all-church events on each campus, either providing the same event at both places or rotating certain events between campuses.

The most difficult "us and them" challenge for most churches is not in-house, not this campus versus that one or the youth group versus the senior adults. The most difficult "us and them" challenge is the one between the church and the community around the church.

Even in a church that has, for many years, sought to be an open-door kind of place, human nature still occasionally prompts "us and them" thinking. For instance, one good-intentioned member suggested to us a few years ago that the church provide tickets to members and regular attenders that would give them the first shot at seats on Christmas Eve and Easter. It wasn't a joke, but an honest suggestion.

It takes continual vision-casting on the part of pastoral leadership to remind a church that they are not called to be an enclave who exists in hostility against the larger community, but called to be a cross-roads for all people in the community, where we all together might be transformed.

Birthing Is More Painful for Some Than for Others

Prospective first-time mothers really have little clue as to what their unique experience of childbirth will be like. When our son was born, the water broke around 6 A.M. on Sunday morning. Jonathan entered the world just after 6 P.M. Monday night. That factors out to a thirty-six-hour labor. Not fun. Not romantic. Not sweet. My sister, on the other hand, has had two babies that practically leapt out of her before she could stop what she was doing and get to the hospital. Still not fun. Still very uncomfortable. But a piece of cake in contrast. These radically different experiences in childbirth parallel the range of experiences church leaders share when it comes to birthing new life and new ways of life into their churches. It's never easy. It's occasionally fun. But sometimes, it's sheer hell. And it isn't fair that it is so much harder some places than others. That's just the way it is.

Jesus never said it would be easy. In fact, he gave every indication that sheer hell is more the norm than easy childbirth in the world of ministry. His first generation of protegees learned that suffering in ministry did not end at Calvary. Consider this little snapshot from a day in the life of the first century apostles from Acts 5:40-42:

> And when they had called in the apostles, they had them flogged. Then they ordered them not to speak in the name of Jesus, and let them go. As they left the council, they rejoiced that they were considered worthy to suffer dishonor for the sake of the name. And every day in the temple and at home they did not cease to teach and proclaim Jesus as the Messiah.

They suffered. They praised God. And they kept on. And they set for us the model of how it works. This passage is provocative in the way it encourages us to give thanks for the times when we have it tougher than our brothers and sisters in the church down the street. Finally, ministry is about more than leadership. It's about more than reaching new people. It's about more than building strong Christian communities. In the end, it's about walking with Jesus. There is nothing sentimental about walking with Jesus. His road is a road of suffering. But it is an honor indeed, to be invited to walk on such a road.

In November 1998, a group of friends and I went down below street level in modern Jerusalem and saw the original Via Delorosa. For several of our group, this was a life-changing experience, to actually stand on the road where Jesus walked as he suffered for the sins of us all. I got on my knees, and touched those precious bricks. I thanked God that, in some small way, I had been privileged to suffer trying to do the work of ministry—that in some minute way, I had been able to walk on this road with Jesus. He was so alone the day he walked that road. But we are never alone on that road, because he walks it with us. That is the deepest honor that we can know in this life, to share in the suffering of Jesus. In doing the work of Jesus wherever God places us, there will be suffering, there will be conflict, and there will be opposition. It will strain our families. It will strain our sanity. It may, at times, strain our health. But if we remember what it is we are doing, we can indeed rejoice in our suffering, and continue on.

My father, Larry Nixon, was in his own day and in his own way, a transformational pastor. The stress of ministry, the conflict and suffering of it, sent him to heart by-pass surgery at the ages of thirty-six, forty-one, and forty-nine. I watched him every step of the road. He never backed off what he honestly felt was the will of God. And God did mighty things in and around his life. When I saw that road underneath Jerusalem, spiritually speaking, it was as much Larry Nixon's road as it was Jesus' road.

One day when I was fifteen, I informed my dad that God had called me to be a pastor. He was very encouraging to me, but later that same day, I later found out, he had a fight with God. Essentially he said, "Oh God, you asked this of me and I gave it, but must you require it of him as well?" He knew what ministry was about. At the time, I found it curious that he was so reserved in his response to me. A quarter century later, I chuckle and I understand. He knew what I was getting into, that's all.

So many critical battles had been won at Gulf Breeze Church before I ever got there. Herb Sadler was a suffering servant through several of those battles. The changes and difficult form of ministry that I know, and the one most loaded with possibilities for suffering for leaders and their families. Your way may be harder than mine was.

Nonetheless, it is a holy and awesome thing that you are doing, if you are leading a church to discover a new way of life, with doors opened wide to serve the world. You are on a road whose bricks have been worn smooth by the feet of saints who have traveled with Jesus before you. I pray that you might not walk in fear of failure, or of conflict, but in courage. Rejoice that God has called you to such a walk. Believe that his purposes will prevail, even if you get fired or fall to an early grave without seeing the full fruits of your labor.

CHAPTER EIGHT

The Stories Yet to Be Written

There are three challenges that I wish to extend. The first is a challenge to your church, wherever it may be, and to every church. The second challenge is to church leaders, who, in reading the preceding chapters, may have caught a vision for the building of a community center. The final challenge is to those of you whom God is calling to start new churches.

The First Challenge

First, I would challenge your church to move toward becoming more of a village church and less of a fortress. This move will require leadership from the pastor(s). Where the pastor catches such a vision and passion, almost any church can begin moving in this direction. So to the pastors of established churches, to the leadership teams of such churches, and to prospective pastors and leaders of such churches, ask yourselves, "What are the components of the village church concept that I resonate with? What are the things that scare me away?" Look back at the characteristics of a village church in chapter one. Which community is your church called to serve? How are you getting to know that community?

Here are a few ways to learn your community.

1. Consider running a demographic study on the territory that your church serves, in order to look objectively at the unique people mix that God has given to your community.

2. Make a list of the various people groups that you can find around you. List the racial/ethnic groupings. List the social groupings, the civic clubs, the street gangs, the generational groupings. List the top hobbies. There are so many kinds of people groups, far beyond ethnic lines. You could keep a list on the wall of the fellowship hall going for weeks and invite anyone to add another group as they think of them.

3. In an urban environment, take your leadership team on an afternoon walk through the immediate neighborhood around the church facility. Hop in the church van or a couple of SUV's and ride up and down streets together in a two-mile radius. Talk to one another about what you are seeing. Add to the list in the fellowship hall.

4. Pray over the list, and begin talking to the people who are part of the various groups. Listen to what they say about their needs and interests. Do more listening than talking.

5. Where those conversations catch fire, begin to partner with those folks in ministry. Don't feel like you need to run seven directions at once. Take on one or two new ministry initiatives with specific people groups.

6. Then, continue to cast the vision that your church is called to be a village church. Offer a set of five to seven core values that reflect the heart of who your church is called to be. These values will help to clarify, confirm, and occasionally redirect a church's mission initiatives. Teach the values, and in so doing, you offer your people the boundaries within which they are free to change the world. Within the boundaries of your values, challenge your people to go for it. Tell them they don't have to wait until there is money in the budget or until the church meets to approve their idea. If it's within the scope of the church's vision and within the church's values, they can give any ministry a shot. Allow ministry to proliferate as it bubbles up from people's passions and callings.

Many people, perhaps most, will just stare at you at first. Don't worry about that. Love those people, but look past them for the eyes that sparkle. Nurture the sparkling eyes.

They are the dreamers, the people who are starting to "get it." Many of the others will catch on in time.

7. Commit your vision and mission to writing. The mission needs to cook for a while before it is committed to the stationery and church bulletin. It needs to grow in the hearts of the pastor and the leaders. If we write it down too early, we will often not be bold enough, or we may create resistance that is based upon misunderstanding and fear. If leaders come back from a retreat and simply announce, "This is the new vision," a church can be needlessly divided. So allow a little time for the consensus to emerge among the leaders. In time, a synergy may develop among the leaders to produce a more focused mission. If we quietly work our vision and develop our sense of mission, we will gather momentum and accumulate allies, some of whom may not have earlier been part of the church. Then, when we finally write the mission down, there will be more consensus. And after we write it down, the result will be a snowball effect. Ministry will begin breaking out in every direction.

The two things that any good church mission statement must do are (1) to lead us to reach beyond ourselves, and (2) to lead us to make disciples. The fewer words it takes us to state how we are called to do the above two things, the better. Also, a pastor needs a personal mission statement that enables her or him to lead with purpose. That mission needs to grow in dialogue with the leadership team that God draws together. Then, it needs to be lived out. It needs to be expressed in teaching and preaching. Purposeful churches are led by purposeful pastors.

So this is the first challenge: to lead established churches to embrace the larger villages in which they live. This challenge is for all of us, leaders of churches large and small!

The Second Challenge

The second challenge is not for everybody. This challenge is directed to leaders of churches who have the resources and/or the holy imagination to bite off the creation of a community center to serve the larger villages of people that God has placed around you. Whether we create such centers on new campuses or we redevelop existing property, there are hundreds of church leaders who will read this book who could create a thing comparable to the Community Life Center in their own communities. Note that I say comparable, not similar. Unless you have a community identical in every way to my community, you will certainly need to create a different kind of community center than we created. The key will be creating a center that meets the perceived needs of people in your community and effectively connects those people with a spiritual community. People's perceived needs may not be their greatest needs. But unless people perceive a need, they seldom will do anything about it. If the church is offering answers to questions people aren't asking, or solutions to problems that people haven't yet identified, or ministries dealing with issues that are not on the front burner in people's lives, the church will fail. So an effective community center must offer activities that will bring the people out, and draw them into community with each other. In my community, recreation is the key. In your community, social services and recovery groups may be the key. In every case, the challenge is to create a community center in which the people served are also effectively invited to and included in the spiritual community. The leaders of a Christian community center must truly burn with the desire that the people they serve meet Christ and be drawn into worship and discipleship groups. Without this intense desire, a church may simply end up with a church-based YMCA or social service center, and nothing more.

I believe in the next decades, literally hundreds of church-based community centers could emerge across North America, renewing both churches and the various communities those churches serve. In most cases, the churches that create effective community centers will be the spiritual leaders in their communities, with powerful influence for good at every level of life.

Is God calling your church to play such a role in the life of your community? If God is calling your church to such a role, be assured that God will provide a way to get from here to wherever it is you are called to go. Don't assume that the price tag is beyond your church's reach! There are enormous untapped resources within most churches and most communities. If money is the issue that is blocking your vision, spend a day with a good stewardship consultant and survey the possibilities and the possible large-gift donors who could help bring your church's visions to life, if only they caught those visions.

The Third Challenge

The final challenge I wish to offer is to persons whom God is calling to start new churches. Most of the great churches of the twenty-first century have not yet been born. That is an exciting truth! In most cases, the pastors haven't even been born yet! But a few pastors have been born, and are approaching the moment when God would have them to birth a new community of faith. If you are one of those pastors, I hope that what you have found in these pages energizes you for the task ahead of you. A capable pastor can usually accomplish more starting from scratch than in trying to butt heads with leaders of established churches.

The sky is the limit in a new church. There are few rules. There are sometimes handcuffing limitations that are attached to the seed money given to start the new church. Denominations are notorious about predetermining a church's location and organizational structure. In many cases, start-up pastors are wiser to work without denominational support than to work with their hands tied. One of the main reasons that new churches so often out-perform established churches is because they take a fresh approach to ministry. Born outside the box, they can think outside the box. After ten years of accumulated tradition and the construction of a facility, most churches begin losing the innovative edge they possessed at their birth. So, if you are starting a church, seize the moment! Think way outside the box to how church is supposed to be. Assume almost nothing except the Bible. Design everything around the personality and needs of the people who live in the community.

In the case of a new church, the church could be conceived as a community center from day one. Alliances could be formed with other faith groups or non-profits in designing and raising support to build a facility whose first purpose is to serve the community. Covenants could be drawn up so that the church has first rights to adequate space in the facility each day in order to offer a seven-day-a-week ministry presence. Allies would share costs, including their share of the capital fund campaign, and share space. Other space could be rented to various entities who fit into the overall vision for the facility and who each buy in to that vision. These could range from restaurants to a health club to a nightclub to a post office to an adult education center to a daycare center to a small bank branch. These vendors could be for-profit or not-for-profit. If they were for-profit, their rent could subsidize the costs of other ministry. My point: if you are starting from scratch, think BIG! You have the potential of creating something that will transform a community.

But My Community Is Not Like Gulf Breeze, Florida!

It is easy to cite the differences between the communities that churches serve, and miss the possibilities for transferring lessons learned from one church to another. Glide Memorial United Methodist Church is the village church for the Tenderloin District in San Francisco. It would be easy for me to look at the Tenderloin District and see the poverty, the prostitution, and the homelessness and say, "That is nothing like my neighborhood. Therefore I can learn nothing from Glide Memorial." Glide is not only on the opposite side of

North America from Gulf Breeze, it is opposite in almost every sort of way from Gulf Breeze. Their community context for ministry is about as different as you could find from the community context where I work. Their theology is different. Their people are different. The pressing community needs are different. And yet, I've learned as much from Glide about how to reach and serve a relatively affluent beach community 2,500 miles away as I have from any other cutting-edge ministry in the United States. If you are unfamiliar with that remarkable congregation, skip over to *www.glide.org* and take a trip to San Francisco for half an hour. You will discover a church radically committed to each of the characteristics of a village church that we examined in chapter two. You will also discover a church where lives are being transformed, where people without hope or dignity are discovering spiritual resurrection.

The community I serve offers an extremely limited population base for what we are trying to do. Churches in more urban settings may have more diverse people groups, but they also have the benefit of many times the number of potential people who could be served at their site.

Any church in any community can choose to be a village church. Any church. Any church in any community can offer hospitality, hope, and healing to people, and those people will respond, regardless of language, ethnicity, or socioeconomic status. We just have to be willing to start with people where we find them.

Too often, churches use their challenging community contexts as an excuse for failure. Too often, churches look at their communities, and turn inward for lack of knowing what else to do. To those churches, I would say building a fortress is not an option. With a bit of Hollywood hyperbole, the nuns in the 1991 film *Sister Act* represented millions of traditional church members, doing their own thing behind the walls of their spiritual fortresses, oblivious to the hopes and hurts and life concerns of the people around them. When Jesus gave us the mandate for existence as churches, he did not offer us the option of "spiritual fortress" as one of our models for ministry. He said, "Go into all the world." He said "Lose your life for my sake and you will find it." What part of *GO* do we not understand?

Let's consider, briefly, several different types of communities where God is wanting to grow spiritual villages.

Changing Communities

Every community is changing. Culture is constantly changing. There are churches in my community who are circling their wagons and refusing to acknowledge the changing needs and the changing look of our area's residents. There are churches in your community doing the same thing. Where there is a migration of new people groups with different language or skin color into a geographic area, the dynamic of change becomes more obvious still. Christianity has been mixing up people from different cultures from day one, when, at Pentecost, everyone on the streets of Jerusalem heard Peter's words *in their own language.*

There are the formal, spoken languages. There are also dialects of languages. There are musical languages. There are cultural languages. In changing communities, we are always faced with new languages. We must find leaders who can speak the good news in the languages of the various people. We must also learn new languages ourselves. It is not enough simply to import someone who can *talk to those people.* If we need to import a leader, we should approach it as importing a leader who can *teach us to talk* with our neighbors, *and to listen* to our neighbors. For example, if a church has worship in both English and Spanish, or if both languages are widely spoken in the surrounding community, there is value in teaching simple English and Spanish in all Sunday school classes and other small groups. This is good for both the groups that are primarily Spanish-speaking and the groups that are primarily English-speaking. Building community is the point. In such a church, the primary sense of fellowship will happen within the groups with a common language. But as those groups learn to talk to one another, in simple, "Good morning, how are you today" ways, Pentecost begins to happen.

There are examples in cities all over the world in which multiple language groups share a common physical center of spiritual community, worship in different rooms at different hours, with the occasional bilingual event to tie the community together. A church should not automatically conclude, when its community changes, that it is time to sell the building and relocate.

However, sometimes it is far better for a church of cultural group "A" to transfer their property to a church of cultural group "B," especially if the members of "A" fail to reach the new community residents, and the members of "A" themselves move to another community and simply commute back to the old neighborhood for an hour on Sunday. In that case, for 165 hours a week, the building is locked, and the only thing happening at the church is the peeling of the paint. Or, maybe the members allow social ministries to be run out of the facility during the week. But if they do not serve the new community groups spiritually, they need to move on.

In the last year, I have consulted with three different large congregations where I have recommended that they relocate their facilities. In one case, a church had overgrown its two acres of land, and had dreams of a much bigger ministry than could ever be accomplished on that spot. I challenged them to sell their property to a smaller church and relocate at the edge of town. In another case, a church of very middle-class folks was located in a community where the homes started at $500,000. The costs of bringing their facility up to par so that it could effectively serve the immediate community were staggering. The restrictions being placed on that church by the township authorities were precluding adequate development of their site. I recommended they consider razing their buildings in order to develop their thirteen acres into million-dollar home sites.

This would provide the funds needed for them to relocate to a much larger parcel of land, where they would be better positioned to reach the masses God has equipped them to reach. In still another situation, a neighborhood population had changed from Anglo to primarily Hispanic and Korean. In this case, a vital Christian community center was needed in their location. But the question was whether or not the present church was the group best suited to maximize the potential for ministry on that spot. My conclusion was that the community would be best served by transferring the management of that site to a growing Korean or Hispanic congregation that could be built into a megachurch. I recommended that the present congregation sell their facility to such a group and move their base of ministry toward the geographical center of the people that they were already reaching, several miles to the north. In every case, I challenged the church to be a community center. However, each of these churches needed to relocate in order to most effectively do this.

When I was in seminary, I did a study comparing Southern Baptists and United Methodists between 1960 and 1980 in southwest Dallas County, Texas. This community, largely known as Oak Cliff, underwent enormous ethnic changes during this twenty-year period. The Southern Baptists responded by relocating many of their Anglo congregations toward the south, where the white residents were moving. A few congregations relocated twice in this twenty-year period of white flight. During this same time frame, all of the United Methodist congregations stayed put. In terms of average Sunday morning attendance within the territory, I found that the Baptists and the Methodists fared exactly the same. Both declined slightly. It did not matter whether they ran from the changing city or tried to change with the city. All the money and energy the Southern Baptists spent on relocation yielded no advantage in terms of the number of people served. Statistically speaking, if we consider only denominational growth, all the moving and running and massive capital fund-raising would appear to have been a total waste. Had the Baptists relaxed like the Methodists did, they probably would have declined by about the same number, without all the added effort of moving. However, upon closer examination, almost every site abandoned by the Southern Baptists was handed over to a different church who was more effective in serving the neighborhood than the departing congregation. The combination of the new sites that the Baptists built in the suburbs and the old sites that were handed over to new churches and groups equaled a greater number of total congregations than before the Baptists moved. Because of this, many more people were reached for Christ as a result of the Baptists relocating than were reached as a result of the Methodists staying put.

I love to see a congregation decide to "stick it out" in a changing neighborhood. But staying with a changing neighborhood only makes sense, when (a) the church is committed *and able* to do what it takes to effectively serve that neighborhood and disciple its people or (b) the church's location is central to the larger region from which it is drawing people. If neither of these conditions is present, there is nothing lost in relocating. In many cases, relocation allows another church a shot at developing a village church at that site. In some cases, a mission partnership can be forged between the church moving out and the church moving in.

Extremely Diverse Communities

In some communities, the issue is not so much change as it is the extreme diversity of people groups. A church may be reaching and serving one or two of the groups quite effectively. It may be, however, that God is leading such a church to "increase its band-width," to communicate the good news to a wider array of people. This church will then create ministries that are responsive to the needs and tastes of a new group of people. Indigenous leadership is absolutely essential. The more varied a community, the more varied the staff and leadership of a church must be.

Often, "indigenous leadership" is interpreted by established congregations to mean getting a Spanish-speaking pastor to lead a tiny band of worshipers in the chapel while the English-speaking pastor leads the service in the sanctuary. The pastor of the Anglo congregation might be paid up to twenty times what the bi-vocational Hispanic pastor is paid. And we wonder why the Hispanic mission never can break beyond forty in average attendance. If a church really wants to reach the Spanish-speaking population (or any language population), it needs to invest in the most capable pastor that can be found. Maybe bi-vocational, maybe full-time. But there needs to be pay equity at least to the level of what the church would pay an English-speaking associate pastor. We must make the same investment in that ministry's music leadership that we would make if we were starting a new music ministry in English. If we want a service to succeed in any language, the music has to be excellent. The new group should be included in the life and leadership of the church, and given prime time and space for classes, ministries, and worship services.

Think about the commitment that Gulf Breeze Church made to the start of its first East Campus worship service. For the first year, we collected less than one dollar for every two we spent at the East Campus. The main reason for this was because we were paying a premium for worship leaders. The church wanted the service to hit 500 in average attendance within the first couple years, so they invested appropriately. We will grow the new people in their stewardship to the place where Main Campus will no longer have to subsidize the East Campus. But I can tell you this for sure: had Main Campus not been willing to pay the cost of providing competent worship leadership at the East Campus, we might have been running 125 in attendance after two years at the Community Life Center rather than 500. This principle holds for almost any new worship community we wish to create. If we are serious about any endeavor, we must be serious about funding for leadership.

Whenever I see a congregation with only one worship service in an area with high diversity of people, I get concerned. I can respect and understand that some churches are called by God to minister to certain niches within the population. But why stop with only one niche in a community setting where it would be possible to serve two or three niches? Now, if you are serving one niche, and the people are responding in such volume that Sundays are filled with multiple worship services, which are packed full, and weekdays are filled with various ministries, I can more easily see the case for a one-track ministry. But when you are serving one niche of people for three hours a week and then leaving the sanctuary empty for the next 141 hours, I wonder, "What is going on here? Why are these people not using their facilities at multiple hours to serve the varied constituencies of their community?"

Highly Secular Communities

People tell me that Gulf Breeze Church has an easier time because it is located in the Bible Belt. For the life of me, I cannot figure out what, exactly, the Bible Belt is. There are more people affiliated with churches per capita in Bismarck, North Dakota, than in Gulf Breeze, Florida, but no one thinks of Bismarck as the Bible Belt. True, there are theological differences between Gulf Breeze and Bismarck. The average person in the South is more likely to take the Bible literally than their cousins up north. Due to the influence of evangelical churches, the average person in the South is probably more likely to understand the Christian faith as involving a personal relationship with God. I am not sure whether the average person in the South is more likely to attend church on any given week or to pray on any given day. Most Southern churches are just as annoying and irrelevant to the life experience and needs of the average twenty-five-year-old as are Northern churches. My best estimate is that only about ten percent of twenty-five-year-olds in my community are "churched," by any meaningful measure. Granted, it may be only three percent in Seattle. But in terms of the percentage of the young adult population that is unchurched, we are talking about ninety percent versus ninety-seven. Christendom niceties aside, most young Americans are unchurched, period.

Many of the people we reach at the Community Life Center have an attitude toward *church* that has to be overcome. They hate church. Or they have had a very painful and negative experience of church. Yet, they tend to believe in God before they come to us. Ninety-six percent of Americans say they believe in God. Atheists are really a very small group in most communities.

I believe that one of the reasons why our church does so well pulling people in from outside organized religion is the fact that Gulf Breeze has *more unchurched people* per capita than other communities around us. Within the Alabama-West Florida Conference of The United Methodist Church, a territory that reaches from central Alabama to the Gulf Coast, including the Florida panhandle, the most secularized communities lie along the beach. We are one of those communities. People along the coast are far less disposed to include church in their life than the people sixty miles inland. However, the only area in the Alabama-West Florida Conference where our churches are collectively growing is along the coast. If you look across the United States, what do the following churches have in common: Saddleback Church, Willow Creek Church, Brooklyn Tabernacle, and Cincinnati Vineyard? One common thread among these churches is orthodoxy in their understanding of who Jesus is. Another common thread is that they have each grown like crazy: they are pace setters among American churches. Another common thread is that each of these churches are located in *highly secularized communities*.

If I could go right now to start a church—just leave this manuscript on my desk for someone else to finish—where would I go? I would go to as secular a city as I could find. I would go to Los Angeles. I would go to Chicago. I would go to Seattle. I would go to New York. Why? Well, in the crudest possible terms, these are untapped markets, with untold millions of human beings who have hopes and hurts that can best be addressed by Jesus Christ. The greatest ministries of the twenty-first century will be built in secular cities.

Highly Churched Communities

Highly churched communities offer, without a doubt, the most difficult setting for a church to do great things for God. If the majority of people are already engaged in a congregation's life to some degree, it becomes harder to garner the momentum to do anything like what has been described in this book.

The best counsel that I could offer a pastor or a congregation in a highly churched community would be to study the community in order to find the population groups that are falling through the cracks of organized religion. Then zero in on those groups that you feel you have a shot at reaching. Don't just go for the same people that the two churches down the street are going for. Look for the people the churches down the street are not engaging. Then be different. In a very conservative community with lots of fundamental churches, create a place where people can safely ask questions. In a very traditional community where every church seems to be singing gospel hymns, put together a band that can sing music that is so edgy that you are certain they would be kicked out of half the churches in your area. Then open the windows and let them play.

If your church's facility is located in an area that is being served effectively by several other churches, each of whom seem to be better than you in some major facet of ministry, you might consider relocating to another area. Rather than trying to compete to get anyone's attention, move your church into a zip code with a lower per capita income and declare yourself a mission outpost. Only a few churches have made such a gutsy move. The results are almost always positive. Talk about a big, hairy, audacious goal: selling out and intentionally moving to a neighborhood in crisis is a giant leap of faith. That will rally people and wake them up, both in the church and in the neighborhood. You may be amazed how affordable the real estate is in many of the neighborhoods that most desperately need ministry in your city.

No Growth Communities

Next to the over-churched community, the next most difficult setting for ministry is the no-growth community, or the community in population decline. Most communities with an agricultural economy across the United States are in population decline. Most cities in the industrial northeast are in population decline. Many central city neighborhoods are in population decline. Ministry is going to look and feel different in such places.

Without as many people moving in, churches in such regions may have less new blood coming into leadership. This can lead to burnout and stagnation among leadership, adversely impacting innovation and outreach. Leaders in such churches can become negative and controlling. Churches in such areas often begin having lots of funerals. Funerals are not all bad. On one hand, it is sad to have to say good-bye to saints who have been our partners in ministry for many decades. On the other hand, most churches have few, if any, problems that a few strategic funerals cannot fix. When the old man dies who once said, "I will die before guitars are played in this church," we need to buy guitars with the proceeds from his memorial gifts. We need to seize the opportunities created by his absence and the end of his controlling.

Let them roll over in their graves. As negative and fearful people kick on out of here, seize the opportunities! Do, however, try to contain your glee at the graveside.

It may be helpful to try to discern the new churches God is building up within the old churches that are passing away. In no-growth communities, the church may well be smaller and leaner a decade from now than it is today. However, it may also be younger and much more Christ-focused ten years from now. It may, in fact, look and feel like a new church ten years from now.

Begin asking, "What kind of church is God bringing to birth here for the future?" Think of the new ministry almost as you would a church start. Retain pastoral leadership who can relate to the old guard even as you bring in the pastor for the church that you are going to bring to life in the next ten years.

In stagnant or declining communities, remember that most area churches will be stagnant or declining. The energy level in most of the worship services in town will be so low as to be undetectable in many instances. This is the backdrop against which you do ministry. Highly energized ministries do well in these areas, in part because they are such a marked contrast to the dying churches all around them.

Virtual Communities

Even in a community with a declining local population, the sky is the limit when you take away geographical constraints. Virtual churches are about to explode onto the scene as major players in the spiritual economy. They will gather people from all walks of life from all over the planet. They will make wonderful relationships possible. They will develop systems of accountability and spiritual nurturing. They will provide excellent teaching. They will fill homes and automobiles with moving and motivational Christian music. There are a host of innovative leaders, most under the age of twenty-five, presently in the process of reinventing church in ways that will affect us in the future in the same way we were affected after the invention of the printing press 550 years ago.

A Christian community center does not have to have a building, just a well-oiled website that connects people based upon a myriad of interests and needs. All the values contained in this book and expressed via the Community Life Center could easily be harnessed in the creation of a web-based community. They that have ears to hear, let them hear! Let them lose sleep tonight as God fills their minds with the possibilities, far beyond anything that this computer-challenged author can imagine.

Generation Y Communities

The last type of community I wish to address involves a group who may have the greatest difficulty resonating with this book. As a pastor, an author, and a human being, I come at all these issues from the perspective of a person born in 1962. That places me on the tail end of the baby boom and at the headwaters of Generation X. Like pastors before me, I will probably now have to work harder and harder to see life through the eyes of the emerging generations of young adults. The way that I see things may look increasingly odd to them. The lessons I learned early in my ministry were taught in a ministry laboratory where baby boomers were the dominant generational group. The highly programmatic ways that Gulf Breeze Church has lived out its mission and values reflects the times in which we have lived and the outlook that we brought to those times.

If you were born after 1980, you may have rolled your eyes in chapter three when I talked about three handshakes and three smiles for every guest. That may seem very canned, even a bit cynical to you. There have probably been other things in the book that struck you as odd or demonstrated to you ways in which Gulf Breeze Church still "doesn't quite get it." I fully expect this to be the case. Because there are always ways in which we don't "get it." No church ever totally gets it.

What I would ask of you, the young reader, is that you look past that which strikes you as a bit goofy and awkward in the application of this book's principles. Look to the principles themselves. Look hard at the concept of what it means to be a village church. Look hard at the components of hospitality, hope, and healing. Glean what is enduring; trash the rest.

Most deeply, I believe that as these principles and values are imbedded in new generations of church leaders, incredible stories will be written which will far outshine anything I have been able to relay in these pages.

In Every Setting, Some Things Are The Same

1. We need to form alliances with other groups and agencies. The church can never be encased in an institution. What God wants and needs to do on the street corner where your church is located is more than what your church alone can do. We need to recognize our allies in the community, the people and groups who are working for common goals. Some of these groups may be explicitly faith-based, others less so.

One plus one plus one does not equal three. It often equals four or five or more. Where multiple groups come together, often there is a synergy that enables the groups to accomplish exponentially more working together than if they were each working in isolation.

Moreover, there is seldom a need to reinvent outstanding systems for delivering care and help to those who need it. Where possible, churches should consider partnership with other groups with compatible visions and missions. Some of these groups have specialized in certain kinds of work and can pursue it with an excellence that is far beyond what the church could presently sponsor directly. If such a partnership distracts the church from the spiritual nature of its mission, then the partnership should not be pursued. But if the partnership brings together various entities for a more united and comprehensive approach in serving a community, then the partnership is a splendid idea.

2. *We need to forge and nurture a vision community in every church.* One leader cannot carry it. It takes a community of leaders. One person can function as leader of the vision community, but that leader cannot carry the vision alone, or even fully conceive the vision alone. There need to be people who are of one accord with the leader or pastor, who share in a covenant together to pray and listen for God's direction for the ministry. If we try to accomplish this without a vision community, if we try to ask one solitary pastor to carry this on her shoulders, mental illness will become a good possibility for that pastor. A pastor functions as the primary spokesperson on behalf of the vision, but a pastor cannot keep the vision stoked within himself. That requires a team. In the New Testament there was always a team. There were elders. There were apostles. Rarely is there any reference to who the senior pastor is at any of the first century churches. We have to read between the lines to guess at that. These first churches were in fact pastored by vision communities, not by individuals.

When a pastor is launching a new ministry or a new direction in ministry, she can cast the vision to potential leaders and see whose eyes sparkle. He can then look to discover the particular gifts among the committed core of leaders, asking, "Which of these gifts do we need in our vision community?" The vision community needs to gather at least monthly to dream and to pray. They can also function as a leadership team or executive committee for the church. Eventually, they can write and renew statements of mission or vision or values for the church. In a church turn around, the vision community and the elected leadership may not be the same groups at first. It is important, however, that within three years that these groups overlap.

The vision community is responsible that the church's vision be cast far and wide. From this vision casting will come almost all the resources of labor and money to do the things God is calling the church to accomplish.

3. Leadership has to fall in love with the neighborhood. Or they need to find a neighborhood (local, regional, or virtual) that they can fall in love with. You can always tell a church that loves its neighborhood. I can feel it as an outsider when I walk in the doors of that church. I guarantee you that the neighbors can feel five times whatever I feel. They know. I don't care what we say on the bulletin or on the church sign. People know when they are loved. If our leaders haven't fallen in love with the people God has sent to our communities, it's time to ask some hard questions behind closed doors. The leaders who catch a vision of what God can do in the neighborhood probably belong at the heart of the vision community.

4. People indigenous to the local village need to be in leadership. It is important that there be leaders who look like (and think like) the community the church serves. These leaders are not figureheads; they are real decision makers whose perspectives and convictions are weighed seriously. They may be staff or lay leadership. But without indigenous leaders, most churches will have difficulty making disciples of the people in their communities. This is not simply an issue of ethnicity. Churches need leaders that reflect the variety of generational groupings in the community as well. They need also to reflect a balance of gender. If we are going to err, let's err toward naming leaders who look more like the community than the present congregation. In most churches, worship leaders are the highest visibility leaders. They do not all need to be indigenous to the local community. Sometimes, teaching pastors or worship pastors from other cultures are very effective in tuning in to where people are in a new culture. I watched my father master the secular culture of Southern California in the 1970s. He was from the backwoods of south Louisiana. His worship leader, however, was a native of Southern California. For these cross-cultural pastors and leaders, it is almost as if their ministry is offered in a second language. Nevertheless,

243

it is important that most highly visible leaders be reflective of the local community in obvious ways.

5. *We need to pray.* There has never been a church built worth more than ten cents that was not built on a foundation of prayer. Without prayer, all the ideas and concepts in this book might as well turn to ash. When leaders and churches are praying, they are constantly offering God the opportunity to form their values and their vision.

In many churches, prayer is perfunctory. It is window dressing. It is what the pastor does before meetings are called to order. But it does not extend to the root. The great churches of our day will all tell you that prayer is a serious matter. These churches care what God thinks. They are ready to go where God leads. They are ready to set aside their will and their pride. And these churches expect a word from God.

When a new pastor's feet hit the pavement in a new pastoral assignment, he usually starts with a heavy agenda of actions to be accomplished. Sometimes, she starts by simply listening and asking questions. The best way to start a new pastorate is to declare a season of fervent prayer for God's vision to be revealed to the church. All the data gathering, all the self-study, and all the dreaming must be bathed in prayer.

6. *We need to be ready to take a little flack.* In my reading of the book of Acts, I am made aware of how normal it is for people who are out on the edge, where God is moving, to be perceived as a threat to other people who have a more settled approach to faith. Much of the persecution in Acts was within the life of the synagogues. It was good people turning on other good people. Whenever God has brought renewal to his people, whether in the first century, the sixteenth century, or the twentieth century, there always seem to be certain family members who just don't get it. Somebody always seems to get bent out of shape when God begins working in our common life.

When that happens to us, we can rest assured that we stand in very good company. And it will happen to us almost as surely as birth, death, and taxes will happen to us. If we seek to lead churches where God is going, somebody will to be ready to burn us in effigy, or worse. The first time it ever happened to me, it was a woman named *Grace*, of all things. I would have counted her as one of my ten favorite people in that church. I liked her wit, I liked her outlook on life, and I liked her style. I genuinely liked this woman. But as I sought to be faithful in leading the church where I was appointed toward transformation, the decision was made to move her Sunday school class in order to make way for an enlarged church nursery. The leaders of Grace's Sunday school class shared in this decision. Nevertheless, Grace got angry with *me*. Our relationship was broken. I was unable to repair it. I still shake my head in amazement about that. I didn't want to be enemies with Grace. I liked Grace!

When division happens, we should not be surprised. It will happen with the nicest of people. Sometimes there will be twenty or thirty people like Grace. And they literally run the would-be transformational pastor out of town. It happens every day. We learn what we can from the experience and we start again in another place with another people.

If There Was Only One Person You Could Talk to about What Is in This Book . . .

Who would it be? If this book has struck a chord with you (or a nerve), consider putting it in the hand of a person you trust and getting their take on it. Pass it on to a fellow ministry team member from your church. Pass it on to a leader in your community who may not even be a part of your church. Say, "I am interested in doing something like this right here in our town. After you read this book, I would like to pick your brain." If you wished, you could share the book with each member of your church's leadership team, and then convene them to reflect on what they read.

Ask one another these questions:

1. What is it that most excited you about this book?
2. Did you get any wild-haired ideas about ministry in your community while reading this book? If so, what were they?
3. Do you believe that the idea of a village church is a relevant concept for your community in the twenty-first century? Why or why not?
4. Do you resonate with the themes of hospitality, hope, and healing? Why or why not? Do you sense that a major component of the Christian mission is missing from this trilogy? Or does this capture the fullness of the good news?
5. Can you envision your church becoming a community center? What are the primary obstacles in the way of this happening? What would it take to overcome these obstacles?
6. Do you feel personally *ready* to lead your church to fling open its doors, even at the cost of some conflict and dissension in the church? What might it take to get ready?
7. What idea in this book would the people you serve find most shocking or subversive? What is your opinion of that idea?
8. What do you think was the most difficult task that Gulf Breeze faced? Deciding to go "two campus"? Creating an open door policy in the first place? Coloring outside the lines of the denomination's standard practices? Attracting leaders and building a leadership team? Raising money?
9. Who are the two or three other people you know who would enjoy reading this book?

A Closing Prayer

For surely I know the plans I have for you, says the LORD, plans for your welfare and not for harm, to give you a future with hope. Then when you call upon me and come and pray to me, I will hear you. When you search for me, you will find me; if you seek me with all your heart, I will let you find me, says the LORD, and I will restore your fortunes and gather you from all the nations and all the places where I have driven you, says the LORD, and I will bring you back to the place from which I sent you into exile. (Jeremiah 29:11-14)

O God, your village is simply enormous, your *kindom* expansive far beyond the vistas of our experience. You have been in the business of tearing down walls and flinging open doors for many centuries. We are awed by the opportunity to intersect our lives with your life and to be part of what you are doing in our communities and in our world. For too long we have played church games that stopped short of the work you have called us to. For too long we have contented ourselves with mediocrity in ministry while the world around us has languished in sin and despair. We hear your calling to be a church for the whole world, to be a center of community for the whole village. Lord, this day, we open our doors. We open them wide, so that all the people of our village might be able to enter them and to experience the good news enfleshed among us. Grant us courage to hold these doors open even if all hell endeavor against us to close them. Grant us courage to give our churches away to all the people for whom Jesus died. And grant us the grace to rejoice with all the angels of heaven over each repentant child of yours who, in traveling through these doors, discovers and accepts the new life you give. Amen.